**Fodor's** POC[...]

# munich

Excerpted from *Fodor's Germany*

fodor's travel publications
new york · toronto · london · sydney · auckland
www.fodors.com

# contents

## maps

# ON THE ROAD WITH FODOR'S

**EVERY TRIP IS A SIGNIFICANT TRIP.** Acutely aware of that fact, we've pulled out all stops in preparing Fodor's Pocket Munich. To guide you in putting together your Munich experience, we've created multiday itineraries and regional tours. And to direct you to the places that are truly worth your time and money, we've enlisted a writer who's seen all the corners of Munich.

**ROBERT TILLEY** landed in Germany more than 25 years ago via Central Africa, South Africa, and England, intending to stay a year before settling somewhere really civilized (his German wife convinced him to stay). He runs a media company in Munich and writes and produces programs for German TV from a lakeside hideaway in the Bavarian Alps.

## Don't Forget to Write

Keeping a travel guide fresh and up-to-date is a big job. So we love your feedback—positive and negative—and follow up on all suggestions. Contact the Munich editor at editors@fodors.com or c/o Fodor's, 280 Park Avenue, New York, New York 10017. And have a wonderful trip!

Karen Cure

*Editorial Director*

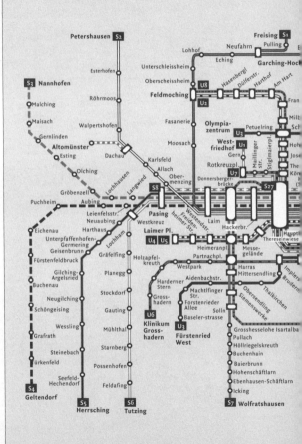

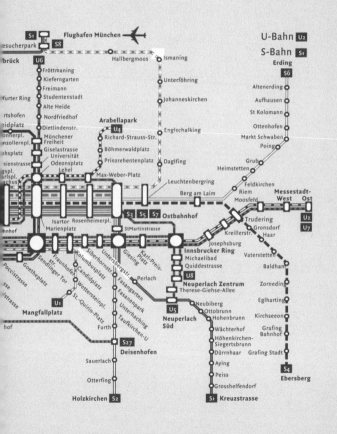

# munich

## In This Section

# introducing munich

## WELCOME TO MUNICH

**MUNICH—MÜNCHEN TO THE GERMANS**—third-largest city in the Federal Republic and capital of the Free State of Bavaria, is the single most popular tourist destination for Germans. This one statistic attests to the enduring appeal of what by any standard is a supremely likable city. Munich is kitsch and class, vulgarity and elegance. It's a city of ravishing rococo and smoky beer cellars, of soaring Gothic and sparkling shops, of pale stucco buildings and space-age factories, of millionaires and lederhosen-clad farmers. Germany's favorite city is a place with extraordinary ambience and a vibrant lifestyle all its own, in a splendid setting within view—on a clear day—of the towering Alps.

Munich belongs to the relaxed and sunny south. Call it Germany with a southern exposure—although it may be an exaggeration to claim, as some Bavarians do, that Munich is the only Italian city north of the Alps. Still, there's no mistaking the carefree spirit that infuses the city, and its easygoing approach to life, liberty, and the pursuit of happiness, Bavarian style. The Bavarians refer to this positively un-Teutonic joie de vivre as Gemütlichkeit.

What makes Munich so special? One explanation is the flair for the fanciful that is deeply rooted in Bavarian culture. And no historical figure better personifies this tradition than Ludwig II, one of the last of the Wittelsbachs, the royal dynasty that for almost 750 years ruled over Munich and southern Germany, until the monarchy was forced to abdicate in 1918. While Bismarck was striving from his Berlin power base to create a modern unified Germany, "Mad" Ludwig—also nicknamed the "Dream King"—was almost bankrupting the state's treasury by building a succession of fairy-tale castles and remote summer retreats in the mountains and countryside.

Munich bills itself as *Die Weltstadt mit Herz* (the cosmopolitan city with heart), which it most assuredly is. A survey suggests that most Germans would prefer to live in Munich than where they currently reside, even though it is probably the most expensive place in reunited Germany. This is not to suggest that all Germans subscribe to the "I Love Munich" concept. Certain buttoned-up types—in Hamburg or Düsseldorf, for example—might look down their imperious noses at Munich as just a mite crass and somewhat tacky, and Bavarians as only a few rungs up from the barbarians. So be it.

Munich's stock image is the cavernous beer hall (such as the world-famous Hofbräuhaus) filled with the deafening echo of a brass oompah band and rows of swaying, burly Bavarians in lederhosen being served by frumpy Fraus in flaring dirndl dresses. Every day in different parts of the city, you'll find scenes like this. But there are also many Müncheners who never step inside a beer hall, who never go near Oktoberfest. They belong to the *other* Munich: a city of charm, refinement, and sophistication, represented by two of the world's most important art galleries and a noted opera house; a city of expensive elegance, where high-fashion shops seem in competition to put the highest price tags on their wares; a city of five-star nouvelle cuisine.

Endowed with vast, green tracts of parks, gardens, and forests; grand boulevards set with remarkable edifices; fountains and statuary; and a river spanned by graceful bridges, Munich is easily Germany's most beautiful and interesting city. If the traveler could visit only one city in Germany, this should be it—

no question. If you factor in the city's dramatic change over the past decade, a traveler who has not visited for awhile might find a whole new Munich has evolved in the interim. For, quietly and without fanfare, Munich has taken its place as the high-tech capital of Germany, developing into the number-one postindustrial-age center in the country and one of the most important cities in Europe. The concentration of electronics and computer firms—Siemens, IBM, Apple, and the like—in and around the city has turned it into the Silicon Valley of Germany.

# PLEASURES AND PASTIMES

## BEER AND BEER GARDENS

Munich has more than 100 beer gardens, ranging from huge establishments that seat several hundred guests to small terraces tucked behind neighborhood pubs and taverns. Beer gardens are such an integral part of Munich life that a council proposal to cut down their hours provoked a storm of protest in 1995, culminating in one of the largest mass demonstrations in the city's history. They open whenever the thermometer creeps above 10°C (42°F) or so and when the sun filters through the chestnut trees that are a necessary part of the beer-garden scenery. Most—but not all—allow you to bring along your own food, and if you do, try not to bring something so foreign as pizza or a burger from McDonald's.

➤ **A BEER GLOSSARY** The alcohol content of German beers varies considerably. At the weaker end of the scale is the light Munich Helles (3.7% alcohol by volume); stronger brews are Pilsner (around 5%) and Doppelbock (more than 7%).

**BOCK:** strong beer, which can be light or dark, sweet or dry.

**DOPPELBOCK:** stronger than Bock, usually dark, and not to be trifled with.

**DUNKLES:** dark beer, often slightly sweeter or maltier than pale (light) beers.

**EXPORT:** usually a pale (light-colored) beer of medium strength.

**HALBE:** half a Mass, the standard beer measure in Bavaria.

**HEFE:** yeast.

**HELLES:** light beer.

**KLAR, KRISTALL:** wheat beer with the yeast removed.

**KLEINES:** a small glass of beer (in Bavaria).

**LAGER:** literally, "store"; that stage of the brewing process when beer matures in the brewery.

**LEICHTBIER:** beer with low alcohol and calorie content, usually pale in color.

**MASS:** a 1-liter (almost 2-pint) glass or earthenware mug.

**NATURTRÜB:** a new term for unfiltered beer, implying the yeast has not been removed.

**OBERGÄRIG:** top-fermented.

**PILS, PILSNER:** a golden-color, dry, bitter-flavored beer named after Pilsen, the Czech town where in the 19th century the brewing style was first developed.

**POLIZEI STUNDE:** literally, "police hour"—closing time; midnight or 1 AM in some big cities, usually earlier in small towns and villages.

**PROST:** German for "cheers."

**RADLER:** lemonade and beer mixed.

**RAUCHBIER:** smoked beer; usually a dark brew with a smoky flavor that comes from infusing the malted barley with beech-wood smoke.

**UNTERGÄRIG:** bottom-fermented.

**WEISSBIER, WEIZENBIER:** wheat beer; a highly carbonated, sharp, and sour brew, often with floating yeast particles.

# DINING

Old Munich restaurants, called *Gaststätten*, feature *gutbürgerliche Küche*, loosely translated as good regional fare, and include brewery restaurants, beer halls, beer gardens, rustic cellar establishments, and *Weinstuben* (wine taverns).

Munich is also a great place for snacks. The city's pre–McDonald's-type fast food is a centuries-old tradition. A tempting array of delectables is available almost anytime day or night; knowing the various Bavarian names will help. The generic term for Munich snacks is *Schmankerl*. And Schmankerl are served at *Brotzeit*, literally translated as "bread time": a snack break, or what the English might call elevenses. According to a saying, *"Brotzeit ist die schönste Zeit"* (snack time is the best time).

In the morning in Munich, one eats *Weisswurst*, a tender minced-veal sausage—made fresh daily, steamed, and served with sweet mustard, a crisp roll or a pretzel, and *Weissbier* (wheat beer). This white sausage is not to everyone's taste, but it is certainly worth trying. As legend has it, this sausage was invented in 1857 by a butcher who had a hangover and mixed the wrong ingredients. A plaque on a wall in Marienplatz marks where the "mistake" was made. It is claimed the genuine article is available only in and around Munich and served only between midnight and noon.

Another favorite Bavarian specialty is *Leberkäs*—literally "liver cheese," although neither liver nor cheese is involved in its construction. It is a spicy meat loaf baked to a crusty turn each morning and served in succulent slabs throughout the day. A *Leberkäs Semmel*—a wedge of the meat loaf between two halves of a crispy bread roll smeared with a bittersweet mustard—is the favorite Munich on-the-hoof snack.

After that comes the repertoire of sausages indigenous to Bavaria, including types from Regensburg and Nürnberg.

More substantial repasts include *Tellerfleisch*, boiled beef with freshly grated horseradish and boiled potatoes on the side, served on wooden plates. (There is a similar dish called *Tafelspitz*.)

Among roasts, *Sauerbraten* (beef) and *Schweinebraten* (pork) are accompanied by dumplings and red cabbage or sauerkraut.

*Haxn* (ham hocks) are roasted until they're crisp on the outside, juicy on the inside. They are served with sauerkraut and potato puree.

You'll also find soups, salads, fish and fowl, cutlets, game in season, casseroles, hearty stews, desserts, and what may well be the greatest variety and the highest quality of baked goods in Europe, including pretzels. In particular, seek out a *Käsestange*— a crispy long bread roll coated in baked cheese. No one need ever go hungry or thirsty in Munich.

## MUSIC AND OPERA

Munich and music complement each other marvelously. The city has two world-renowned orchestras (one, the Philharmonic, is now directed by the American conductor James Levine), the Bavarian State Opera Company, wonderful choral ensembles, two opera houses (the chief of these, the Bavarian State Opera, is managed by an ingenious British director, Peter Jonas), a rococo jewel of a court theater, and a modern Philharmonic concert hall of superb proportions and acoustics—and that's just for starters.

## SHOPPING

Munich has three of Germany's most exclusive shopping streets. At the other end of the scale, it has a variety of flea markets to rival those of any other European city. In between are department stores, where acute German-style competition assures reasonable prices and often produces outstanding bargains. The Christmas markets, which spring up all over the city as November slides into December, draw from backroom-studio artisans and artists with wares of outstanding beauty and originality. Collect their business cards—in the summer you're sure to want to order another of those little gold baubles that were on sale in December.

## QUICK TOURS

If you're here for just a short period you need to plan carefully so as to make the most of your time in Munich. The following itineraries outline major sights throughout the city, and will help you structure your visit efficiently. Each is intended to take about four hours—a perfect way to fill a free morning or afternoon.

### TOUR 1

Start this central Munich tour on Marienplatz square shortly before 11 AM, when the elaborate Glockenspiel (carillon) in the tower of the neo-Gothic Neues Rathaus (city hall) clanks and whirrs into action. There's a tourist information office in the Rathaus, if you need maps and brochures. The city's original city hall, the Altes Rathaus, is on the eastern edge of the square, but you can only admire it from outside. Exit Marienplatz on the south, along the old cattle market, Rindermarkt, and get a bird's eye view of the city from the top of the tower of St. Peter's Church. The city's central market, the Viktualienmarkt, is just south of St. Peter's, and at lunchtime you can sample Munich beer and meat specialties at one of the many market stalls. Stroll down Rosental to Sendlingerstrasse, for the one "must-see" Munich church interior: the incredibly ornate 18th-century Asamkirche. Explore the boutique-crammed jumble of streets behind the church, and within five minutes you'll be in the city's shopping mile, the traffic free Neuhauser-Kaufinger-Strasse mall. Head back east towards Marienplatz, your starting and ending point, but leave time for a visit to the city's cathedral, the Frauenkirche. Its tall brick towers signal the way.

## TOUR 2

Marienplatz is again the starting point. Duck through the arches of the former city hall, the Altes Rathaus, turn left into Burgstrasse, and you'll find a peaceful square lined by medieval buildings that were once the site of the original Wittelsbach royal palace, the Alter Hof. Its successor, the Residenz, is a few hundred yards north. Cross Maximilianstrasse and Max-Josef-Platz (the opera house on your right) to reach it. Exploring the Residenz (closed Monday) will take a couple of hours, but afterwards stroll north to the royal gardens, the Hofgarten. On the way, take a look at the Feldherrnhalle (an imitation Florentine loggia abused as a Nazi shrine) and the Baroque Theatinerkirche. Finish your tour with coffee at Munich's oldest cafe, the Tambosi, on Odeonsplatz.

## TOUR 3

This museum tour starts at the main railway station, the Hauptbahnhof, where there is a tourist information office. Head northwest, through the original botanical gardens, the Alter Botanischer Garten, and continue up Meiserstrasse to Königsplatz. If antiquities are your thing there are two fine museums of Greek, Etruscan and Roman art on either side of the huge square (the Antikensammlungen and the Glyptothek). For something more modern continue up Meiserstrasse, which turns into Arcisstrasse, and on the right you'll find the Alte Pinakothek and Neue Pinakothek, Munich's leading art galleries. Visit Munich's museums in the afternoon, when the school groups have passed through—it will also give you an excuse to end your tour at happy hour in one of the many bars and cafés in this part of Schwabing, the old artists' quarter.

## TOUR 4

Don walking shoes for this tour through Munich's huge city park, the Englischer Garten. Starting point is Odeonsplatz (U3 and U6 subway stop), which leads into the old royal gardens, the

Hofgarten, and thence into the Englischer Garten. On the right as you cross into the park you'll see one of the few remnants of Nazi architecture in Munich—the Haus der Kunst, a major art gallery and home to Munich's top disco, the PI. Return there after dark, if that's your scene, but first introduce yourself to Munich beer at the city's most celebrated beer garden, the Chinesischer Turm (Chinese Tower), named after the replica of a Chinese pagoda that stands incongruously in the midst of leafy English-style parkland. Work up a thirst again with a 1km walk north to the park's largest stretch of water, the Kleinhesselohesee, where you'll find another more upmarket beer garden. Walk around the lake and head south to Odeonsplatz, trying to syncronize this part of your tour with the sunset behind Munich's steepled city panorama.

## In This Section

# here and there

**MUNICH IS A WEALTHY CITY**—and it shows. Everything is extremely upscale and up-to-date. At times the aura of affluence may be all but overpowering. But that's what Munich is all about these days and nights: a new city superimposed on the old; conspicuous consumption; a fresh patina of glitter along with the traditional rustic charms. Such are the dynamics and duality of this fascinating metropolis.

*Numbers in the text correspond to numbers in the margin and on the Munich map.*

## THE CITY CENTER

Munich is unusual among German cities because it has no identifiable, homogeneous Old Town center. Postwar developments often separate clusters of buildings that date back to Munich's origins—and not always to harmonious effect. The outer perimeter of this tour is defined more by your stamina than by ancient city walls.

### A Good Walk

Begin your walk through the city center at the **Hauptbahnhof** ①, the main train station and site of the city tourist office, which is next to the station's main entrance, on Bahnhofplatz. Pick up a detailed city map here. Cross Bahnhofplatz, the square in front of the station (or take the underpass), and walk toward Schützenstrasse, which marks the start of Munich's pedestrian shopping mall, the *Fussgängerzone*, 2 km (1 mi) of traffic-free streets. Running virtually the length of Schützenstrasse is

Munich's largest department store, Hertie. At the end of the street you descend via the pedestrian underpass into another shopping empire, a vast underground complex of boutiques and cafés. Above you is the busy traffic intersection, **Karlsplatz** ②, known locally as the Stachus, with a popular fountain area.

Ahead stands one of the city's oldest gates, the Karlstor, first mentioned in local records in 1302. Beyond it lies Munich's main shopping thoroughfare, Neuhauserstrasse, and its extension, Kaufingerstrasse. On your left as you enter Neuhauserstrasse is another attractive fountain: a late-19th-century figure of Bacchus. This part of town was almost completely destroyed by bombing during World War II and has been extensively rebuilt. Great efforts were made to ensure that the designs of the new buildings harmonized with the old city, although some of the modern structures are little more than functional. Though this may not be an architectural showplace, there are redeeming features to the area. Haus Oberpollinger, on Neuhauserstrasse, is one; it's a department store hiding behind an imposing 19th-century facade. Notice the weather vanes of old merchant ships on its high-gabled roof.

Shopping, however, is not the only attraction on these streets. Worldly department stores rub shoulders with two remarkable churches: the **Bürgersaal** ③ and the **Michaelskirche** ④. The 16th-century Michaelskirche was the first Renaissance church of this size in southern Germany. Its fanciful facade contrasts wonderfully with the baroque exterior of the Bürgersaal. The massive building next to Michaelskirche was once one of Munich's oldest churches, built in the late 13th century for Benedictine monks. It was secularized in the early 19th century, served as a warehouse for some years, and today is the **Deutsches Jagd- und Fischereimuseum** ⑤.

Turn left here onto Augustinerstrasse, and you will soon arrive in Frauenplatz, a quiet square with a shallow, sunken fountain. Towering over it is the **Frauenkirche** ⑥, Munich's cathedral, whose twin domes are the city's main landmark and its symbol. From the cathedral follow any of the alleys heading east, and you'll reach the very heart of Munich, **Marienplatz** ⑦, which is surrounded by stores and dining spots. Marienplatz is dominated by the 19th-century **Neues Rathaus** ⑧; the **Altes Rathaus** ⑨, a medieval building of assured charm, sits modestly, as if forgotten, in a corner of the square.

Hungry? Thirsty? Help is only a few steps away. From the Altes Rathaus, cross the street, passing the Heiliggeistkirche, an early Munich church with a rococo interior added between 1724 and 1730. Heiliggeiststrasse brings you to the jumble known as the **Viktualienmarkt** ⑩, the city's open-air food market, where you can eat a stand-up lunch at any of the many stalls.

From the market follow Rosental into Sendlingerstrasse, one of the city's most interesting shopping streets, and head left toward Sendlinger Tor, a finely restored medieval brick gate. On your right as you head down Sendlingerstrasse is the remarkable **Asamkirche** ⑪. The exterior fits so snugly into the street's housefronts (the architects lived next door) that you might easily overlook the church as you pass.

From the Asamkirche, backtrack up Sendlingerstrasse and turn right onto Rindermarkt (the former cattle market), and you'll be beneath the soaring tower of the **Peterskirche** ⑫, or Alter Peter (Old St. Peter's), the city's oldest and best-loved parish church. From the Peterskirche reenter Marienplatz and pass in front of the Altes Rathaus once again to step into Burgstrasse. You'll soon find yourself in the quiet, airy **Alter Hof** ⑬, the inner courtyard of the original palace of Bavaria's Wittelsbach rulers. A short distance beyond the northern archway of the Alter Hof, on the north side of Pfisterstrasse, stands the former royal mint, the **Münze** ⑭.

If you'd like to visit some museums, extend your walk by about 10 minutes, returning down Burgstrasse to broad Tal, once an important trading route that entered Munich at the Isartor, now beautifully restored to its original medieval appearance.

# munich (münchen)

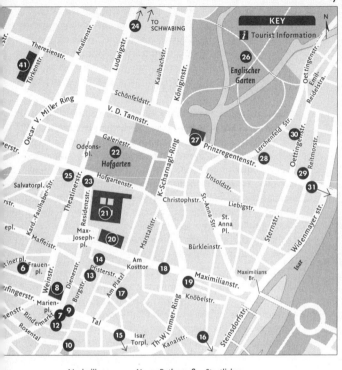

Continue across Isartorplatz into Zweibrückenstrasse, and you'll come to the Isar River. There, on an island in the river, is the massive bulk of the **Deutsches Museum** ⑮, with a gigantic thermometer and barometer on its tower showing the way to the main entrance. Budding scientists and young dreamers will be delighted by its many interactive displays with buttons to push and cranks to turn.

On a sunny day join the locals for ice cream and a stroll along the Isar River, where the more daring sunbathe nude on pebble islands. On a rainy day you can splash around in the Müllersches Volksbad, a restored Jugendstil (art nouveau) indoor swimming pool at Ludwigsbrücke, opposite the Deutsches Museum (one afternoon a week the Volksbad is reserved for the nudists, a very German concession). The soaring organ-pipe-like facade above on the hill above the Volksbad belongs to the modern, redbrick **Gasteig Kulturzentrum** ⑯, home of the Munich Philharmonic Orchestra and a collection of theaters, galleries, and cafés, where your tour can end with a pot of coffee and a pastry.

### TIMING
Set aside at least a whole day for this walk, hitting Marienplatz when the glockenspiel plays at 11 or noon. The churches along the route will each demand at least a half hour of your time. You'll also be tempted by the department stores in the pedestrian zone. Prepare for big crowds in Marienplatz when the glockenspiel plays, and try to avoid shopping between noon and 2, when workers on lunch break make for the department stores. Aficionados of hunting or engineering could spend hours in the Deutsches Jagd- und Fischereimuseum and Deutsches Museum.

## Sights to See

❸ **ALTER HOF** (Old Palace). This palace was the original residence of the Wittelsbachs, the ruling dynasty established in 1180. The palace now serves as local government offices. Something of a medieval flavor survives in the Alter Hof's quiet courtyard in the otherwise busy downtown area. Don't pass through without turning to admire the medieval oriel (bay window) that hides on the south wall, just around the corner as you enter the courtyard.

👋 **⑨ ALTES RATHAUS** (Old City Hall). This was Munich's first city hall, built in 1474. Its great hall—destroyed in 1944 but now fully restored—was the work of architect Jörg von Halspach. It is used for official receptions and is not normally open to the public. The tower provides a satisfyingly atmospheric setting for a **toy museum**, accessible via a winding staircase. It includes several exhibits from the United States. *Marienpl., tel. 089/294–001. Museum DM 5. Daily 10–5:30.*

★ **⑪ ASAMKIRCHE** (Asam Church). Munich's most unusual church has a suitably extraordinary entrance, framed by raw rock foundations. The insignificant church door, crammed between its craggy shoulders, gives little idea of the splendor within. Above the doorway St. Nepomuk, a 14th-century Bohemian monk who drowned in the Danube, is being led by angels from a rocky riverbank to heaven. The 18th-century church's official name is Church of St. Johann Nepomuk, but it is known as the Asamkirche for its architects, the brothers Cosmas Damian and Egid Quirin Asam. Inside you'll discover a prime example of true southern German, late-baroque architecture. Frescoes and rosy marble cover the walls, from which statuary and gilding explode—there's even a gilt skeleton at the sanctuary's portal. For such a small church (there are only 12 rows of pews), the opulence and lavish detailing are overwhelming. *Sendlingerstr. Daily 9–5:30.*

**③ BÜRGERSAAL** (Citizens' Hall). Beneath the modest roof of this unassuming church are two contrasting levels. The Oberkirche (upper level)—the church proper—is a richly decorated baroque oratory. Its elaborate stucco foliage and paintings of Bavarian places of pilgrimage project a distinctly different ambience from that of the Unterkirche (lower level), reached by a double staircase. This gloomy, cryptlike chamber contains the tomb of Rupert Mayer, a famous Jesuit priest renowned for his energetic and outspoken opposition to the Nazis. *Neuhauserstr. 14, tel. 089/223–884. Oberkirche Mon.–Sat. 11–1, Sun. 9–12:30; Unterkirche Mon.–Sat. 6:30 AM–7 PM, Sun. 7–7.*

**⑤ DEUTSCHES JAGD- UND FISCHEREIMUSEUM** (German Museum of Hunting and Fishing). Lovers of the thrill of the chase will be fascinated by this museum. It contains the world's largest collection of fishhooks, some 500 stuffed animals (including a 6½-ft-tall North American grizzly bear), a 12,000-year-old skeleton of an Irish deer, and a valuable collection of hunting weapons. *Neuhauserstr. 2, tel. 089/220–522. DM 5. Tues., Wed., and Fri.–Sun. 9:30–5; Mon. and Thurs. 9:30–9.*

**★ ✋ ⑮ DEUTSCHES MUSEUM** (German Museum of Science and Technology). Within a monumental building next to the Isar River, this museum—filled with aircraft, vehicles, locomotives, and machinery—is an engineering student's dream. Nineteen kilometers (12 miles) of corridors, six floors of exhibits, and 30 departments make up the immense collections. Not all exhibits have explanations in English, which is why you should skip the otherwise impressive coal-mine labyrinth. The most technically advanced planetarium in Europe, it has up to six shows daily, including a Laser Magic display. An IMAX theater—a wraparound screen six stories high—shows nature and adventure films. The Internet Café on the third floor is open daily 9–3. To arrange for a two-hour tour in English, call 089/2179–252 two weeks in advance. *Museumsinsel 1, tel. 089/21790; 089/211–25180 to reserve tickets at planetarium and IMAX. Museum DM 10, Planetarium DM 12.50, IMAX DM 11.90; combined ticket for planetarium and IMAX DM 20.50 (admission for some performances is higher). Daily 9 AM–11 PM. www.fdt.de*

**OFF THE BEATEN PATH** **FRANZISKANERKLOSTERKIRCHE ST. ANNA (Franciscan Monastery Church of St. Anne)** – This striking example of the two Asam brothers' work is in the Lehel district. Though less opulently decorated than the Asamkirche, this small Franciscan monastery church, consecrated in 1737, impresses with its sense of movement and its heroic scale. It was largely rebuilt after wartime bomb damage. The ceiling fresco by Cosmas Damian Asam was removed before World War II and, after restoration, now glows in all its original vivid joyfulness. The ornate altar was also designed by the Asam brothers. Towering over the delicate little church, on the opposite side of the street, is the neo-Romanesque bulk of the 19th-century church of St. Anne. You can get to Lehel on Tram 17 or U-bahn 4 or 5 from the city center. *St.-Anna-Str., tel. 089/212–1820.*

★ ⑥ **FRAUENKIRCHE** (Church of Our Lady). Munich's Dom (cathedral) is a distinctive late-Gothic brick structure with two enormous towers that are Munich's chief landmark. Each is more than 300 ft high, and both are capped by very un-Gothic onion-shape domes. The towers have become the symbol of Munich's skyline— some say because they look like overflowing beer mugs.

The main body of the cathedral was completed in 20 years (1474–94)—a record time in those days. The towers were added, almost as an afterthought, in 1524–25. Jörg von Polling, the Frauenkirche's original architect, is buried here. The building suffered severe damage during the Allied bombing of Munich and was lovingly restored between 1947 and 1957. Inside, the church combines most of von Polling's original features with a stark, clean modernity and simplicity of line, emphasized by slender, white octagonal pillars that sweep up through the nave to the tracery ceiling far above. As you enter the church, look on the stone floor for the dark imprint of a large foot—the *Teufelstritt* (Devil's Footprint). According to local lore, the devil challenged von Polling to build a nave without windows. Von Polling wagered his soul and accepted the challenge, building a cathedral that is flooded with light from 66-ft-high windows that are invisible to anyone standing at the spot marked by the

Teufelstritt. The cathedral houses an elaborate 15th-century black-marble memorial to Emperor Ludwig the Bavarian, guarded by four 16th-century armored knights.

A splendid view of the city is yours from an observation platform high up in one of the towers. But beware—you must climb 86 steps to reach the tower elevator! *Frauenpl., tel. 089/290–0820. Tower DM 4. Tower elevator Apr.–Oct., Mon.–Sat. 10–5.*

**16 GASTEIG KULTURZENTRUM** (Gasteig Culture Center). This striking postmodern, brick cultural complex for music, theater, and film has an open-plan interior and a maze of interior courtyards and plazas, sitting high above the Isar River. The center has two theaters, where plays in English are occasionally staged. *Rosenheimerstr. 5, tel. 089/480–980.*

**1 HAUPTBAHNHOF** (Main Train Station). The city tourist office here has maps and helpful information on events around town. *Bahnhofpl., tel. 089/2333–0258.*

**2 KARLSPLATZ.** Known locally as the Stachus, this busy intersection has one of Munich's most popular fountains, a circle of water jets that acts as a magnet on hot summer days for city shoppers and office workers seeking a cool place to relax. A semicircle of yellow-front buildings with high windows and delicate cast-iron balconies back the fountain.

★ **7 MARIENPLATZ.** Bordering the ☞ **Neues Rathaus**, shops, and cafés, this square is named after the gilded statue of the Virgin Mary that has watched over it for more than three centuries. It was erected in 1638 at the behest of Elector Maximilian I as an act of thanksgiving for the city's survival during the Thirty Years' War, the cataclysmic religious struggle that devastated vast regions of Germany. When the statue was taken down from its marble column for cleaning in 1960, workmen found a small casket in the base containing a splinter of wood said to be from the cross of Christ. *Bounded by Kaufingerstr., Rosenstr., Weinstr., and Dienerstr.*

**❹ MICHAELSKIRCHE** (St. Michael's Church). A curious story explains why this sturdy Renaissance church has no tower. Seven years after the start of construction the principal tower collapsed. Its patron, pious Duke Wilhelm V, regarded the disaster as a heavenly sign that the church wasn't big enough, so he ordered a change in the plans—this time without a tower. Completed seven years later, the Michaelskirche was the first Renaissance church of this size in southern Germany. The duke is buried in the crypt, along with 40 other Wittelsbachs, including the eccentric King Ludwig II. A severe neoclassical monument in the north transept contains the tomb of Napoléon's stepson, Eugene de Beauharnais, who married one of the daughters of King Maximilian I and died in Munich in 1824. You'll find the plain white-stucco interior of the church and its slightly barnlike atmosphere soothingly simple after the lavish decoration of the nearby Bürgersaal. *Neuhauserstr. 6, tel. 089/5519–9257. DM 2. Weekdays 10–1 and 2–4:30, Sat. 10–3. Closed Sun. and public holidays.*

**⓮ MÜNZE** (Mint). Originally the royal stables, the Münze was created by court architect Wilhelm Egkl between 1563 and 1567 and now serves as an office building. A stern neoclassical facade emblazoned with gold was added in 1809; the interior courtyard has Renaissance-style arches. *Pfisterstr. 4. Free. Mon.–Thurs. 8–4, Fri. 8–2.*

**❽ NEUES RATHAUS** (New City Hall). Munich's present city hall was built between 1867 and 1908 in the fussy, turreted, neo-Gothic style so beloved by King Ludwig II. Architectural historians are divided over its merits, though its dramatic scale and lavish detailing are impressive. Perhaps the most serious criticism is that the Dutch and Flemish style of the building seems out of place amid the baroque and rococo of so much of the rest of the city. In 1904 a glockenspiel (a chiming clock with mechanical figures) was added to the tower; it plays daily at 11 AM, noon, and 9 PM, with an additional performance at 5 PM June–October. As chimes peal out over the square, the clock's doors flip open and brightly colored dancers and jousting knights go through their paces. They act out two events from Munich's past: a tournament held in Marienplatz in 1568 and the *Schäfflertanz* (Dance of the Coopers), which commemorated the end of the plague of 1517. When Munich was in ruins after the war, an American soldier contributed some paint to restore the battered figures, and he was rewarded with a ride on one of the jousters' horses, high above the cheering crowds. You, too, can travel up there, by elevator, to an observation point near the top of one of the towers. On a clear day the view is spectacular. *Marienpl., tel. 089/2331. Tower DM 3. Mon.–Thurs. 9–4, Fri. 9–1.*

**⑫ PETERSKIRCHE** (St. Peter's Church). Munich's oldest and smallest parish church traces its origins to the 11th century and over the years has been restored in a variety of architectural styles. Today you'll find a rich baroque interior, with a magnificent late-Gothic high altar and aisle pillars decorated with exquisite 18th-century figures of the apostles. In clear weather it's well worth the climb up the 300-ft tower—the view includes glimpses of the Alps to the south. The Peterskirche has a Scottish priest who is glad to show English-speaking visitors around. *Rindermarkt, tel. 089/260–4828. Tower DM 2.50. Mon.–Sat. 9–7, Sun. 10–7.*

OFF THE
BEATEN
PATH

**STREETCAR 19** – For the cheapest sightseeing tour of the city center on wheels, board this streetcar outside the ☞ **Hauptbahnhof** on Bahnhofplatz and make the 15-minute journey to Max Weber Platz. Explore the streets around the square, part of the old Bohemian residential area of Haidhausen (with some of the city's best bars and restaurants, many on the villagelike Kirchenstrasse), and then return by a different route on Streetcar 18 to Karlsplatz.

**THERESIENWIESE** – The site of Munich's annual beer festival—the notorious Oktoberfest—is only a 10-minute walk from the ☞ **Hauptbahnhof** or only a single stop away by subway (U-4 or

# Paris, France.

# Paris, Texas.

# When it Comes to Getting Local Currency at an ATM, Same Thing.

Whether you're in Yosemite or Yemen, using your Visa® card or ATM card with the PLUS symbol is the easiest and most convenient way to get local currency. For example, let's say you're in France. When you make a withdrawal, using your secured PIN, it's dispensed in francs, but is debited from your account in U.S. dollars. This makes it easy to take advantage of favorable exchange rates. And if you need help finding one of Visa's 627,000 ATMs in 127 countries worldwide, visit **visa.com/pd/atm**. We'll make finding an ATM as easy as finding the Eiffel Tower, the Pyramids or even the Grand Canyon.

It's Everywhere You Want To Be.

# SEE THE WORLD
# IN FULL COLOR

**Fodor's** Exploring Guides bring all the great sights vividly to life with hundreds of photographs, fascinating historical background, and colorful anecdotes. Detailed maps and practical information keep you headed in the right direction.

Pair a Fodor's Exploring Guide with your trusted Fodor's Pocket Guide for a complete planning package.

U-5). It is an enormous exhibition ground, named after a young woman whose engagement party gave rise to the Oktoberfest. In 1810 the party celebrated the betrothal of Princess Therese von Sachsen-Hildburghausen to the Bavarian crown prince Ludwig, later Ludwig I. It was such a success, attended by nearly the entire population of Munich, that it became an annual affair. Beer was served then as now, but what began as a night out for the locals has become a 16-day international bonanza at the end of September and the beginning of October, attracting more than 6 million people each year (it qualifies as an *Oktoberfest* by ending the first Sunday in October).

Overlooking the Theresienwiese is a 19th-century hall of fame— one of the last works of Ludwig I—and a monumental bronze statue of the maiden **Bavaria,** more than 100 ft high. The statue is hollow, and 130 steps take you up into the braided head for a view of Munich through Bavaria's eyes. DM 4. *Dec.–Oct., Tues.– Sun. 10–noon and 2–4.*

★ ⑩ **VIKTUALIENMARKT.** The city's open-air food market (*Viktualien* means vittles) has a wide range of produce, German and international foodstuffs, and tables and counters for eating and drinking, which make the area a feast for the eyes as well as the stomach. It's also the realm of the garrulous, sturdy market women who run the stalls with dictatorial authority. Whether here, or at a bakery, *do not* try to select your pickings by hand; ask for help.

## ROYAL MUNICH

From the relatively modest palace of the Alter Hof (☞ City Center, *above*), Munich's royal rulers expanded their quarters northward, where more space was to be found than in the jumble of narrow streets of the old quarter. The Wittelsbachs built a palace more suitable for their regal pretensions and laid out a fine garden, at first off limits to all but the nobility. Three splendid avenues radiated outward from this new center of royal rule, and fine homes arose along them. One of them—Prinzregentenstrasse—marks the southern end of Munich's huge public park, the Englischer Garten—also the creation of a Wittelsbach ruler.

## A Good Walk

A good way to start this very long walk is to stoke up with a Bavarian breakfast of Weisswurst, pretzels, and beer at the **Hofbräuhaus** ⑰, perhaps Munich's best-known beer hall, on Am Platzl. Turn right from the Hofbräuhaus for the short walk along Orlandostrasse to **Maximilianstrasse** ⑱, Munich's most elegant shopping street, named after King Maximilian II, whose statue you'll see far down on the right. This wide boulevard has many grand buildings, which contain government offices and the city's ethnological museum, the **Staatliches Museum für Völkerkunde** ⑲. The Maximilianeum, on a rise beyond the Isar River, is an impressive mid-19th-century palace where the Bavarian state government now meets.

Across Maximilianstrasse as you enter from the Hofbräuhaus stands a handsome city landmark: the Hotel Vier Jahreszeiten, a historic host to traveling princes, millionaires, and the expense-account jet set.

Turn left down Maximilianstrasse, away from the Maximilianeum, and you'll enter the square called Max-Joseph-Platz, dominated by the pillared portico of the 19th-century **Nationaltheater** ⑳, home of the Bavarian State Opera Company. The statue in the square's center is of Bavaria's first king, Max Joseph. Along the north side of this untidily arranged square (marred by the entrance to an underground parking lot) is the lofty and austere south wall of the **Residenz** ㉑, the royal palace of Wittelsbach rulers for more than six centuries.

Directly north of the Residenz, on Hofgartenstrasse, lies the former royal garden, the **Hofgarten** ㉒. You can be forgiven for any confusion about your whereabouts ("Can this really be Germany?") when you step from the Hofgarten onto Odeonsplatz. To your left is the 19th-century **Feldherrnhalle** ㉓, modeled after the familiar Loggia dei Lanzi in Florence. Looking north up Ludwigstrasse, the arrow-straight avenue that begins at the Feldherrnhalle, you'll see the **Siegestor** ㉔, or victory arch, which marks the beginning of Leopoldstrasse. Completing this impressively Italianate panorama is the great yellow bulk of the former royal church of St. Kajetan, the **Theatinerkirche** ㉕, an imposing baroque structure across from the Feldherrnhalle.

Now head north up Ludwigstrasse. The first stretch of the street was designed by court architect Leo von Klenze. In much the same way that Baron Haussmann would later demolish many of the old streets and buildings in Paris, replacing them with stately boulevards, von Klenze swept aside the small dwellings and alleys that stood here to build his great avenue. His high-windowed and formal buildings have never quite been accepted by Müncheners. Most people either love it or hate it. Von Klenze's buildings end just before Ludwigstrasse becomes Leopoldstrasse, and it is easy to see where he handed construction over to another leading architect, Friedrich von Gärtner. The severe neoclassical buildings that line southern Ludwigstrasse—including the Bayerische Staatsbibliothek (Bavarian State Library), the Universität (University), and the peculiarly Byzantine Ludwigskirche—fragment into the lighter styles of Leopoldstrasse. The more delicate structures are echoed by the busy street life you'll find here in summer. Once the hub of the legendary artists' district of Schwabing, Leopoldstrasse still throbs with life from spring to fall, exuding the atmosphere of a Mediterranean boulevard, with cafés, wine terraces, and artists' stalls. In comparison, Ludwigstrasse is inhabited by ghosts of the past.

At the south end of Leopoldstrasse lies the great open quadrangle of the university. A circular area divides into two piazzas named after anti-Nazi resistance leaders: Geschwister-Scholl-Platz and Professor-Huber-Platz. The Scholls, brother and sister, and Professor Huber were members of the short-lived resistance movement known as the Weisse Rose (White Rose) and were executed after show trials. At its north end, Leopoldstrasse leads into Schwabing itself, once Munich's bohemian quarter but now distinctly upscale. Explore the streets of old Schwabing around Wedekindplatz to get the feel of the place. (Those in search of the bohemian mood that once animated Schwabing should head to Haidhausen, on the other side of the Isar.)

Bordering the east side of Schwabing is the **Englischer Garten** ㉖. Five kilometers (3 miles) long and 1½ km (about 1 mi) wide, it's Germany's largest city park, stretching from Prinzregentenstrasse, the broad avenue laid out by Prince Regent Luitpold at the end of the 19th century, to the city's northern boundary, where the lush parkland is taken over by the rough embrace of open countryside. Dominating the park's southern border is one of the few examples of Hitler-era architecture still standing in Munich: the colonnaded **Haus der Kunst** ㉗, a leading art gallery and home to Munich's most fashionable nightclub, the PI.

A few hundred yards farther along Prinzregentenstrasse are two other leading museums, the **Bayerisches Nationalmuseum** ㉘ and the **Schack-Galerie** ㉙, while around the first left-hand corner, on Lerchenfeldstrasse, is a museum of prehistory, the **Prähistorische Staatssammlung** ㉚, that brings to life the ancient past.

The column you see standing triumphant on a hill at the eastern end of Prinzregentenstrasse, just across the Isar River from the Schack-Galerie, is Munich's well-loved Friedensengel (Angel of Peace). This striking gilt angel crowns a marble column in a small park overlooking the Isar River. Just across the river, beyond the Friedensengel, is another historic home that became a major Munich art gallery—the **Museum Villa Stuck** ③, a jewel of Art-Nouveau fantasy.

There are innumerable walks along the banks of the Isar River and in the nearby Englischer Garten, where you can stop at one of its four beer gardens (the Chinese Tower is the largest and most popular) or visit the Seehaus, on the shore of the park's lake, the Kleinhesseloher See. Here you'll have another choice to make: a smart restaurant or a cozy *Bierstube* (beer tavern).

**TIMING**

You'll need a day (and good walking shoes) for this stroll, which ends in the Englischer Garten. Set aside at least two hours for a tour of the Residenz. If the weather is good, return to the southern end of the Englischer Garten at dusk, when you'll be treated to an unforgettable silhouette of the Munich skyline, black against the retreating light.

## Sights to See

**❷⓼ BAYERISCHES NATIONALMUSEUM** (Bavarian National Museum). The extensive collection here contains Bavarian and other German art and artifacts. The highlight for some will be the medieval and Renaissance wood carvings, with many works by the great Renaissance sculptor Tilman Riemenschneider. Tapestries, arms and armor, a unique collection of Christmas crèches (the Krippenschau), Bavarian arts and crafts, and folk artifacts compete for your attention. Although the museum places emphasis on Bavarian cultural history, it has artifacts of outstanding international importance and regular exhibitions that attract worldwide attention. *Prinzregentenstr. 3, tel. 089/211–241. DM 3, DM 8 for special exhibitions. Tues.–Sun. 9:30–5.*

★ **❷⓺ ENGLISCHER GARTEN** (English Garden). This virtually endless park, which is embraced by open countryside at Munich's northern city limits, was designed for the Bavarian prince Karl Theodor by a refugee from the American War of Independence, Count Rumford. Although Rumford was of English descent, it was the open, informal nature of the park—reminiscent of the rolling parklands with which English aristocrats of the 18th century liked to surround their country homes—that determined its name. It has a boating lake, four beer gardens, and a series of curious decorative and monumental constructions, including the Monopteros, a Greek temple designed by von Klenze for King Ludwig I and built on an artificial hill in the southern section of the park. In the center of the park's most popular beer garden is a Chinese pagoda erected in 1789. It was destroyed during the war and then reconstructed. The Chinese Tower beer garden is world famous, but the park has prettier places for nursing a beer: the Aumeister, for example, along the northern perimeter. The Aumeister's restaurant is in an early 19th-century hunting lodge.

The Englischer Garten is a paradise for joggers, cyclists, and, in winter, cross-country skiers. The Munich Cricket Club grounds are in the southern section—and spectators are welcome. The park has specially designated areas for nude sunbathing—the Germans have a positively pagan attitude toward the sun—so don't be surprised to see naked bodies bordering the flower beds and paths. *Main entrances at Prinzregentenstr. and Koniginstr.*

**㉓ FELDHERRNHALLE** (Generals' Hall). This hall of fame that honors generals who have led Bavarian forces was modeled after the 14th-century Loggia dei Lanzi in Florence. The open-sided pavilionlike building bears two great bronze plaques honoring the generals who led the Bavarian army in three centuries of wars. Larger-than-life statues of two of these generals, Count Johann Tserclaes Tilly, who led Catholic forces in the Thirty Years' War, and Prince Karl Philipp Wrede, hero of the 19th-century Napoleonic Wars, flank two huge Bavarian lions. The imposing structure was turned into a militaristic shrine in the 1930s and '40s by the Nazis, who also found significance in the coincidence that it marked the site of Hitler's abortive coup, or putsch, which took place in 1923. All who passed it had to give the Nazi salute. A tiny alley behind the Feldherrnhalle, linking Residenzstrasse and

Theatinerstrasse and now lined with exclusive boutiques, was used by those who wanted to dodge the tedious routine. *South end of Odeonspl.*

**27** **HAUS DER KUNST** (House of Art). This colonnaded, classical-style building is one of Munich's few remaining examples of Hitler-era architecture and was officially opened by the führer himself. In the Hitler years it showed only work deemed to reflect the Nazi aesthetic. One of its most successful postwar exhibitions was devoted to works banned by the Nazis. It stages exhibitions of art, photography, and sculpture, as well as theatrical and musical "happenings." The disco PI is in the building's west wing. *Prinzregentenstr. 1, tel. 089/211–270. Admission depends on exhibition. Tues.–Sun. 9–5.*

**17** **HOFBRÄUHAUS.** Duke Wilhelm V founded Munich's most famous brewery in 1589. Hofbräu means "royal brew," which aptly describes the golden beer poured in king-size liter mugs. If the cavernous downstairs hall is too noisy for you, try the quiet restaurant upstairs. Americans, Australians, and Italians far outnumber Germans, and the brass band that performs here most days adds modern pop and American folk to the traditional German numbers. *Am Platzl 9, tel. 089/221–676.*

**22** **HOFGARTEN** (Royal Garden). The formal garden was once part of the royal palace grounds. It's bordered on two sides by arcades designed in the 19th century by the royal architect Leo von Klenze. On the east side of the garden stands the new state chancellery, built around the ruins of the 19th-century Army Museum and incorporating the remains of a Renaissance arcade. Its most prominent feature is a large copper dome. Bombed during World War II air raids, the museum stood untouched for almost 40 years as a grim reminder of the war.

In front of the chancellery stands one of Europe's most unusual—some say most effective—war memorials. Instead of looking up at a monument, you are led down to a **sunken crypt** covered by a massive granite block. In the crypt lies a German soldier from World War I. *Hofgartenstr., north of Residenz.*

The monument is a stark contrast to the **memorial** that stands unobtrusively in front of the northern wing of the chancellery: a simple cube of black marble bearing facsimiles of handwritten wartime manifestos by anti-Nazis leaders, including members of the White Rose movement.

**LUDWIGSKIRCHE** (Ludwig's Church). Planted halfway along the severe, neoclassical Ludwigstrasse is this curious neo-Byzantine/early Renaissance–style church. It was built at the behest of Ludwig I to provide his newly completed suburb with a parish church. It's worth a stop to see the fresco of the *Last Judgment* in the choir. At 60 ft by 37 ft, it is one of the world's largest. *Ludwigstr. 22, tel. 089/288–334. Daily 7–7.*

**⓲ MAXIMILIANSTRASSE.** Munich's sophisticated shopping street was named after King Maximilian II, who wanted to break away from the Greek-influenced classical style of city architecture favored by his father, Ludwig I. With the cabinet's approval, he created this broad boulevard, its central stretch lined with majestic buildings (now government offices and the state ethnological museum, the ☞ **Staatliches Museum für Völkerkunde**). It culminates on a rise beyond the Isar River in the stately outlines of the **Maximilianeum,** a lavish 19th-century arcaded palace built for Maximilian II and now the home of the Bavarian state parliament. Only the terrace can be visited.

**㉛ MUSEUM VILLA STUCK.** This museum is the former home of one of Munich's leading turn-of-the-20th-century artists, Franz von Stuck (1863–1928). His work covers the walls of the haunting rooms of the neoclassical villa, which is also used for regular art exhibits organized by the museum's Australian director. *Prinzregentenstr. 60, tel. 089/4555–5125. DM 2 and up, according to exhibit. Tues., Wed., and Fri.–Sun. 10–5; Thurs. 10–8.*

**㉚ NATIONALTHEATER** (National Theater). Built in the late 19th century as a royal opera house with a pillared portico, this large theater was bombed during the war but is now restored to its original splendor. Today's opera house has some of the world's most advanced stage technology. *Max-Joseph-Pl., tel. 089/2185–1920.*

**㉚ PRÄHISTORISCHE STAATSSAMMLUNG** (State Prehistoric Collection). This is Bavaria's principal record of its prehistoric, Roman, and Celtic past. The perfectly preserved body of a ritually sacrificed young girl, recovered from a Bavarian peat moor, is among the more spine-chilling exhibits. Head down to the basement to see the fine Roman mosaic floor. *Lerchenfeldstr. 2, tel. 089/211–2402. DM 5; free Sun. Tues., Wed., and Fri.–Sun. 9–4; Thurs. 9–4 and 7–9.*

★ **㉑ RESIDENZ** (Royal Palace). Munich's royal palace began as a small castle in the 14th century. The Wittelsbach dukes moved here when the tenements of an expanding Munich encroached upon their Alter Hof (☞ City Center, *above*). In succeeding centuries the royal residence developed parallel to the importance, requirements, and interests of its occupants. It came to include the Königsbau (on Max-Josef-Platz) and then (clockwise) the Alte Residenz; the Festsaal (Banquet Hall); the Altes Residenztheater/ Cuvilliés Theater; the now ruined Allerheiligenhofkirche (All Souls' Church); the Residenztheater; and the Nationaltheater.

Building began in 1385 with the **Neuveste** (New Fortress), which comprised the northeast section; most of it burned to the ground in 1750, but one of its finest rooms survived: the 16th-century **Antiquarium,** which was built for Duke Albrecht V's collection of antique statues (today it's used chiefly for state receptions). The throne room of King Ludwig I, the **Neuer Herkulessaal,** is now a concert hall. The accumulated Wittelsbach treasures are on view in several palace museums.

The **Schatzkammer** (treasury; DM 7; Tues.–Sun. 10–4:30) has a rich centerpiece in its small Renaissance statue of St. George, studded with 2,291 diamonds, 209 pearls, and 406 rubies; paintings, tapestries, furniture, and porcelain are housed in the **Residenzmuseum** (DM 7; Tues.–Sun. 10–4:30); antique coins glint in the **Staatliche Münzsammlung** (Residenzstr. 1; DM 4; free Sun.; Tues., Wed., and Fri.–Sun. 10–5; Thurs. 10–6:45); and Egyptian works of art make up the **Staatliche Sammlung Ägyptischer Kunst** (Hofgarten entrance; DM 5, free Sun.; Tues. 9–9, Wed.–Fri. 9–4, weekends 10–5).

In the summer, chamber-music concerts take place in the inner courtyard. Also in the center of the complex is the small rococo **Altes Residenztheater/Cuvilliés Theater** (Residenzstr.; DM 3; Mon.–Sat. 2–5, Sun. 10–5). It was built by François Cuvilliés between 1751 and 1755, and it still holds performances. The French-born Cuvilliés was a dwarf who was admitted to the Bavarian court as a decorative "bauble." Prince Max Emanuel recognized his latent artistic ability and had him trained as an architect. The prince's eye for talent gave Germany some of its richest rococo treasures. *Max-Joseph-Pl. 3, entry through archway at Residenzstr. 1, tel. 089/290–671.*

**㉙ SCHACK-GALERIE.** Those with a taste for florid and romantic 19th-century German paintings will appreciate the collections of the Schack-Galerie, originally the private collection of one Count Schack. Others may find the gallery dull, filled with plodding and repetitive works by painters who now repose in well-deserved obscurity. *Prinzregentenstr. 9, tel. 089/2380–5224. DM 4; free Sun. Wed.–Mon. 10–5.*

**㉔ SIEGESTOR** (Victory Arch). Marking the beginning of Leopoldstrasse, the Siegestor has Italian origins—it was modeled on the Arch of Constantine in Rome—and was built to honor the achievements of the Bavarian army during the Wars of Liberation (1813–15). *Leopoldstr.*

**19 STAATLICHES MUSEUM FÜR VÖLKERKUNDE** (State Museum of Ethnology). Arts and crafts from around the world are displayed in this extensive museum. There are also regular ethnological exhibits. *Maximilianstr. 42, tel. 089/210–1360. DM 6; free Sun. Tues.– Sun. 9:30–4:30.*

**25 THEATINERKIRCHE** (Theatine Church). This mighty baroque church owes its Italian appearance to its founder, Princess Henriette Adelaide, who commissioned it in gratitude for the birth of her son and heir, Max Emanuel, in 1663. A native of Turin, the princess distrusted Bavarian architects and builders and thus summoned a master builder from Bologna, Agostino Barelli, to construct her church. He took as his model the Roman mother church of the newly formed Theatine Order. Barelli worked on the building for 11 years but was dismissed before the project was completed. It was another 100 years before the Theatinerkirche was finished. Its lofty towers frame a restrained facade capped by a massive dome. Step inside to admire its austere, monochrome, stucco interior. *Theatinerstr. 22, tel. 089/210–6960. Daily 7–7:30.*

NEED A
BREAK? Munich's oldest café, **Tambosi** (Odeonspl., tel. 089/298–322) borders the street across from the Theatinerkirche. Watch the hustle and bustle from an outdoor table or retreat through a gate in the Hofgarten's western wall to the café's tree-shaded beer garden. If the weather's cool or rainy, find a corner in the cozy, eclectically furnished interior.

## THE MAXVORSTADT AND SCHWABING

Here is the artistic center of Munich: Schwabing, the old artists' quarter, and the neighboring Maxvorstadt, where most of the city's leading art galleries and museums are congregated. Schwabing is no longer the bohemian area where such diverse residents as Lenin and Kandinsky were once neighbors, but at least the solid cultural foundations of the Maxvorstadt are immutable. Where the two areas meet (in the streets behind the university), life hums with a creative vibrancy that is difficult to detect elsewhere in Munich.

## A Good Walk

Begin with a stroll through the city's old botanical garden, the **Alter Botanischer Garten** ㉜. The grand-looking building opposite the garden's entrance is the Palace of Justice, law courts built in 1897 in suitable awe-inspiring dimensions. On one corner of busy Lenbachplatz, you can't fail to notice one of Munich's most impressive fountains: the monumental late-19th-century Wittelsbacher Brunnen. Beyond the fountain, in Pacellistrasse, is the baroque **Dreifaltigkeitskirche** ㉝.

Leave the garden at its Meiserstrasse exit and continue up the street. On the right-hand side you'll pass two solemn neoclassic buildings closely associated with the Third Reich. The first served as the administrative offices of the Nazi Party in Munich. The neighboring building is the Music Academy, where Hitler, Mussolini, Chamberlain, and Daladier signed the prewar pact that carved up Czechoslovakia.

At the junction of Meiserstrasse and Briennerstrasse, look right to see the obelisk dominating the circular **Karolinenplatz** ㉞. To your left will be the expansive **Königsplatz** ㉟, bordered by two museums, the **Glyptothek** ㊱ and the **Antikensammlungen** ㊲.

After walking by the museums, turn right onto Luisenstrasse, and you'll arrive at a Florentine-style villa, the **Städtische Galerie im Lenbachhaus** ㊳, which has an outstanding painting collection. Continue down Luisenstrasse, turning right on Theresienstrasse to reach Munich's three leading art galleries, the **Alte Pinakothek** ㊴, the **Neue Pinakothek** ㊵, opposite it, and the **Pinakothek der Moderne** ㊶. They are as complementary as their buildings are contrasting: the Alte Pinakothek, severe and serious in style; the Neue Pinakothek, almost frivolously

Florentine; and the Pinakothek der Moderne, glass-and-concrete new.

After a few hours immersed in culture, end your walk with a leisurely stroll through the neighboring streets of Schwabing, which are lined with boutiques, bars, and restaurants. If it's a fine day, head for the **Elisabethmarkt,** Schwabing's permanent market.

### TIMING

This walk may take an entire day, depending on how long you linger at the major museums en route. Avoid the museum crowds by visiting as early in the day as possible. All of Munich seems to discover an interest in art on Sunday, when admission to most municipal and state-funded museums is free; you might want to take this day off from culture and join the late-breakfast and brunch crowd at the Elisabethmarkt, a beer garden, or at any of the many bars and Gaststätten. Some have Sunday-morning jazz concerts. Many Schwabing bars have happy hours between 6 and 8—a relaxing way to end your day.

## Sights to See

★ ❸❾ **ALTE PINAKOTHEK** (Old Picture Gallery). The towering brick Alte Pinakothek was constructed by von Klenze between 1826 and 1836 to exhibit the collection of old masters begun by Duke Wilhelm IV in the 16th century. It's now judged one of the world's great picture galleries. Among its most famous works are Dürers, Rembrandts, Rubenses (the world's largest collection), and two celebrated Murillos. *Barerstr. 27, tel. 089/2380–5216. DM 7; free Sun.; DM 12 for a combined ticket for the Alte Pinakothek and Neue Pinakothek, valid for 2 days. Tues. and Thurs. 10–8; Wed. and Fri.–Sun. 10–5.*

❸❷ **ALTER BOTANISCHER GARTEN** (Old Botanical Garden). Munich's first botanical garden began as the site of a huge glass palace, built in 1853 for Germany's first industrial exhibition. In 1931 it shared the fate of a similarly palatial glass exhibition hall, London's Crystal Palace, when its garden burned to the ground; six years later it was redesigned as a public park. Two features from the 1930s remain: a small, square **exhibition hall**, still used for art shows, and the 1933 **Neptune Fountain,** an enormous work in the heavy, monumental style of the prewar years. At the international electricity exhibition of 1882, the world's first high-tension electricity cable was run from the park to a Bavarian village 48 km (30 mi) away. *Entrance at Lenbachpl.*

NEED A BREAK? On the north edge of the Alter Botanischer Garten is one of the city's central beer gardens. It's part of the **Park-Café** (Sophienstr. 7, tel. 089/598–313), which at night becomes a fashionable nightclub serving magnums of champagne for DM 1,500 apiece. Prices in the beer garden are more realistic.

**37** **ANTIKENSAMMLUNGEN** (Antiquities Collection). This museum at Köningsplatz has a collection of small sculptures, Etruscan art, Greek vases, gold, and glass. *Königspl. 1, tel. 089/598–359. DM 6; combined ticket to Antikensammlungen and Glyptothek DM 10. Tues. and Thurs.–Sun. 10–5; Wed. 10–8; tour every other Wed. at 6.*

**33** **DREIFALTIGKEITSKIRCHE** (Church of the Holy Trinity). A local woman prophesied doom for the city unless a new church was erected: this striking baroque edifice was then promptly built between 1711 and 1718. It has heroic frescoes by Cosmas Damian Asam. *Pacellistr. 10, tel. 089/290–0820. Daily tour DM 5. Daily 7–7.*

**ELISABETHMARKT** (Elisabeth Market). Schwabing's permanent market is smaller than the popular Viktualienmarkt but hardly less colorful. It has a pocket-size beer garden, where a jazz band performs every Saturday from spring to autumn. *Arcistr. and Elisabethstr.*

**36** **GLYPTOTHEK.** Greek and Roman sculptures are on permanent display here. *Königspl. 3, tel. 089/286–100. DM 6; combined ticket to Glyptothek and Antikensammlungen DM 10; free Sun. Tues., Wed., and Fri.–Sun. 10–5; Thurs. 10–8; tour every other Thurs. at 6.*

**34** **KAROLINENPLATZ** (Caroline Square). At the junction of Barerstrasse and Briennerstrasse, this circular area is dominated by an obelisk unveiled in 1812 as a memorial to Bavarians killed fighting Napoléon. **Amerikahaus** (America House) faces Karolinenplatz. It has an extensive library and a year-round program of cultural events. *Karolinenpl. 3, tel. 089/552–5370.*

**35** **KÖNIGSPLATZ** (King's Square). This expansive square is lined on three sides with the monumental Grecian-style buildings by Leo von Klenze that gave Munich the nickname "Athens on the Isar." The two templelike structures are now the ☞ **Antikensammlungen** and the ☞ **Glyptothek** museums. In the 1930s the great parklike square was paved with granite slabs, which resounded with the thud of jackboots as the Nazis commandeered the area for their rallies. Although a busy road passes through it, the square has regained something of the green and peaceful appearance intended by Ludwig I.

**40** **NEUE PINAKOTHEK** (New Picture Gallery). This exhibition space opened in 1981 to house the royal collection of modern art left homeless and scattered after its former building was destroyed in the war. The exterior of the modern building mimics an older one with Italianate influences. The interior offers a magnificent environment for picture gazing, at least partly due to the superb natural light flooding in from the skylights. The highlights of the collection are probably the impressionist and other French 19th-century works—Monet, Degas, and Manet are all well represented. But there's also a substantial collection of 19th-century German and Scandinavian paintings—misty landscapes predominate— that are only now coming to be recognized as admirable products of their time. *Barerstr. 29, tel. 089/2380–5195. DM 7; free Sun. Tues. and Thurs.–Sun. 10–5; Wed. 10–8.*

**41** **PINAKOTHEK DER MODERNE.** Munich's ever-delayed new museum is scheduled to open between summer and October 2001. Five outstanding art and architectural collections once distributed in separate, inadequate quarters will be joined in a striking glass-and-concrete complex: galleries of modern art, industrial and graphic design, the Bavarian State collection of graphic art, and the Technical University's architectural museum. *Türkenstr. at Gabelsbergerstr., and Luisenstr. at Theresienstr., tel. 089/238–05118. Admission fees and opening hrs unavailable at press time.*

**38 STÄDTISCHE GALERIE IM LENBACHHAUS** (Municipal Gallery). You'll find an internationally renowned picture collection inside a delightful late-19th-century Florentine-style villa, former home and studio of the artist Franz von Lenbach (1836–1904). It contains a rich collection of works from the Gothic period to the present, including an exciting assemblage of art from the early 20th-century *Blaue Reiter* (Blue Rider) group: Kandinsky, Klee, Jawlensky, Macke, Marc, and Münter. *Luisenstr. 33, tel. 089/233–0320. DM 10. Tues.–Sun. 10–6.*

## OUTSIDE THE CENTER

**BMW MUSEUM.** Munich is the home of the famous car firm, and its museum contains a dazzling collection of BMWs old and new. It adjoins the BMW factory on the eastern edge of the ☞ **Olympiapark.** You can't miss this museum, a circular tower that looks as if it served as a set for *Star Wars. Petuelring 130, U-bahn 3 to Petuelring, tel. 089/3822–3307. DM 5.50. Daily 9–5, last entry at 4.*

**BOTANISCHER GARTEN** (Botanical Garden). A collection of 14,000 plants, including orchids, cacti, cycads, Alpine flowers, and rhododendrons, makes up one of the most extensive botanical gardens in Europe. The garden lies on the eastern edge of ☞ **Schloss Nymphenburg** park. Take Tram 17 or Bus 41 from the city center. *Menzingerstr. 65, tel. 089/1786–1350. DM 4. Oct.–Mar., daily 9–noon and 2–4:30; Apr.–Sept. daily 9–7:30; hothouses daily 9–noon and 1–4.*

**GEISELGASTEIG MOVIE STUDIOS.** Munich is Germany's leading moviemaking center, and the local Hollywood-style lot,

Geiselgasteig, is on the southern outskirts of the city. The Filmexpress transports you on a 1½-hour tour of the sets of *Das Boot* (The Boat), *Die Unendliche Geschichte* (The Neverending Story), and other productions. Stunt shows are held at 11:30, 1, and 2:30 and action movies are screened in Showscan, the super-wide-screen cinema. Take U-bahn 1 or 2 from the city center to Silberhornstrasse and then change to Tram 25 to Bavariafilmplatz. A combined ticket for a family of up to five persons, covering public transport and entry to the studios, costs DM 45. *Bavariafilmpl. 7, tel. 089/6499–2304. DM 17; stunt show DM 10; Showscan DM 8; combined ticket for studio tour, stunt show, and Showscan cinema DM 31. Nov.–Feb., daily 10–3 (tours only); Mar.–Apr., daily 9–4; May–Oct., daily 9–5.*

🦢 **HELLABRUN ZOO.** There are a minimum of cages and many parklike enclosures at this attractive zoo. The 170 acres include restaurants and children's areas. Take Bus 52 from Marienplatz or U-bahn 3 to Thalkirchen, at the southern edge of the city. *Tierparkstr. 30, tel. 089/625–0834. DM 10. Apr.–Sept., daily 8–6; Oct.–Mar., daily 9–5.*

🦢 **OLYMPIAPARK** (Olympic Park). On the northern edge of Schwabing, undulating circus-tent-like roofs cover the stadiums built for the 1972 Olympic Games. The roofs are made of translucent tiles that glisten in the midday sun and act as amplifiers for the rock concerts held here. Tours of the park are conducted on a Disneyland-style train throughout the day. An elevator will speed you up the 960-ft **Olympia Tower** for a view of the city and the Alps; there's also a revolving restaurant near the top. The former Olympic cycling stadium was converted in 1999 to an **Olympic Spirit** theme park where you can compete or judge in virtual-reality Olympic sports. Take U-bahn 3 to the park. *tel. 089/3067–2414, 089/3066–8585 for restaurant. Olympic Spirit DM 26; tower elevator DM 5. Tours (Apr.–Nov.): grand tour, starting 2 PM, DM 13; stadium tour, starting 11 AM, DM 8. Main stadium daily 9–4:30; Olympic Spirit Sun.–Thurs. 10–7, Fri. and Sat. 10–10; tower daily 9 AM–midnight.*

**SCHLOSS BLUTENBURG.** This medieval palace is the home of an international collection of 500,000 children's books in more than 100 languages. This library is augmented by collections of original manuscripts, illustrations, and posters. The castle chapel, built in 1488 by Duke Sigismund, has some fine 15th-century stained glass. Take any S-bahn train to Pasing station, then Bus 73 or 76 to the castle gate. The palace is beyond Nymphenburg, on the northwest edge of Munich. *Blutenberg 35, tel. 089/811–3132. Free. Weekdays 10–5.*

★ **SCHLOSS NYMPHENBURG.** Five generations of Bavarian royalty spent their summers in this glorious baroque and rococo palace. Nymphenburg is the largest palace of its kind in Germany, stretching more than 1 km (½ mi) from one wing to the other. The palace grew in size and scope over a period of more than 200 years, beginning as a summer residence built on land given by Prince Ferdinand Maria to his beloved wife, Henriette Adelaide, on the occasion of the birth of their son and heir, Max Emanuel, in 1663. The princess hired the Italian architect Agostino Barelli to build both the Theatinerkirche (☞ Royal Munich, *above*)—as an expression of her gratitude for the birth—and the palace, which was completed in 1675 by his successor, Enrico Zuccalli. Within the original building, now the central axis of the palace complex, is a magnificent hall, the **Steinerner Saal**, extending over two floors and richly decorated with stucco and swirling frescoes. In the summer, chamber-music concerts are given here. The decoration of the Steinerner Saal spills over into the surrounding royal chambers, one of which houses the famous **Schönheitsgalerie** (Gallery of Beauties; DM 4). The walls are hung from floor to ceiling with portraits of women who caught the roving eye of Ludwig I, among them a butcher's daughter and an English duchess. The most famous portrait is of Lola Montez, a sultry beauty and high-class courtesan who, after a time as the mistress of Franz Liszt and later Alexandre Dumas, captivated Ludwig I to such an extent that he lost his throne because of her.

The palace is in a park laid out in formal French style, with low hedges and gravel walks extending into woodland. Tucked away among the ancient trees are three fascinating structures. Don't miss the **Amalienburg** hunting lodge, a rococo gem built by François Cuvilliés, architect of the Altes Residenztheater ☞ Royal Munich, *above*). The silver-and-blue stucco of the little Amalienburg creates an atmosphere of courtly high life, making clear that the pleasures of the chase here did not always take place outdoors. In the lavishly appointed kennels you'll see that even the dogs lived in luxury. The **Pagodenburg** was built for royal tea parties. Its elegant French exterior disguises a suitably Asian interior in which exotic teas from India and China were served. Swimming parties were held in the **Badenburg,** Europe's first post-Roman heated pool.

Nymphenburg contains so much of interest that a day hardly provides enough time. Don't leave without visiting the former royal stables, the **Marstallmuseum,** (DM 3), or Museum of Royal Carriages. It houses a fleet of vehicles, including an elaborately decorated sleigh in which King Ludwig II once glided through the Bavarian twilight, postilion torches lighting the way. On the floor above are examples of Nymphenburg porcelain, produced here between 1747 and the 1920s.

A popular museum in the north wing of the palace has nothing to do with the Wittelsbachs but is one of Nymphenburg's major attractions. The **Museum Mensch und Natur** (Museum of Man and Nature; tel. 089/171–382; DM 3, free Sun.; Tues.–Sun. 9–5) concentrates on three areas of interest: the variety of life on Earth, the history of humankind, and our place in the environment. Main exhibits include a huge representation of the human brain and a chunk of Alpine crystal weighing half a ton.

Take Tram 17 or Bus 41 from the city center to the Schloss Nymphenburg stop. *tel. 089/179–080. Schloss Nymphenburg complex (Gesamtkarte, or combined ticket) DM 11. Apr.–Sept., daily 9–*

# Smart Sightseeings

Savvy travelers and others who take their sightseeing seriously have skills worth knowing about.

**DON'T PLAN YOUR VISIT IN YOUR HOTEL ROOM** Don't wait until you pull into town to decide how to spend your days. It's inevitable that there will be much more to see and do than you'll have time for: choose sights in advance.

**ORGANIZE YOUR TOURING** Note the places that most interest you on a map, and visit places that are near each other during the same morning or afternoon.

**START THE DAY WELL EQUIPPED** Leave your hotel in the morning with everything you need for the day—maps, medicines, extra film, your guidebook, rain gear, and another layer of clothing in case the weather turns cooler.

**TOUR MUSEUMS EARLY** If you're there when the doors open you'll have an intimate experience of the collection.

**EASY DOES IT** See museums in the mornings, when you're fresh, and visit sit-down attractions later on. Take breaks before you need them.

**STRIKE UP A CONVERSATION** Only curmudgeons don't respond to a smile and a polite request for information. Most people appreciate your interest in their home town. And your conversations may end up being your most vivid memories.

**GET LOST** When you do, you never know what you'll find—but you can count on it being memorable. Use your guidebook to help you get back on track. Build wandering-around time into every day.

**QUIT BEFORE YOU'RE TIRED** There's no point in seeing that one extra sight if you're too exhausted to enjoy it.

**TAKE YOUR MOTHER'S ADVICE** Go to the bathroom when you have the chance. You never know what lies ahead.

*12:30 and 1:30–5; Oct.–Mar., daily 10–12:30 and 1:30–4. All except Amalienburg and gardens closed Mon.*

**SCHLOSS SCHLEISSHEIM** (Schleissheim Palace). In 1597 Duke Wilhelm V decided to look for a peaceful retreat outside Munich and found what he wanted at this palace, then far beyond the city walls but now only a short ride on a train and a bus. A later ruler, Prince Max Emanuel, added a second, smaller palace, the **Lustheim**. Separated from Schleissheim by a formal garden and a decorative canal, the Lustheim houses Germany's largest collection of Meissen porcelain. To reach the palace, take the suburban S-bahn 1 line (to Oberschleissheim station) and then Bus 292 (which doesn't run on weekends). *Maximilianshof 1, Oberschleissheim, tel. 089/315–5272. Combined ticket for palaces and porcelain collection DM 5. Tues.–Sun. 10–12:30 and 1:30–5.*

**SÜDFRIEDHOF** (Southern Cemetery). At this museum-piece cemetery you'll find many famous names but few tourists. Four hundred years ago it was a graveyard beyond the city walls for plague victims and paupers. During the 19th century it was refashioned into an upscale last resting place by the city architect Friedrich von Gärtner. Royal architect Leo von Klenze designed some of the headstones, and both he and von Gärtner are among the famous names you'll find there. The last burial here took place more than 40 years ago. The Südfriedhof is a short 10-minute walk south from the U-bahn station at Sendlinger-Tor-Platz. *Thalkirchnerstr.*

# eating out

**WITH SEVEN MICHELIN-STARRED** restaurants to its credit, Munich claims to be Germany's gourmet capital. It certainly has an inordinate number of ritzy French restaurants, some with chef-owners who honed their skills under such Gallic masters as Paul Bocuse. Epicureans are convinced that one can dine as well in Munich as in any other city on the Continent. However, for many the true glory of Munich's kitchen artistry is to be experienced in those rustic eating places that serve down-home Bavarian specialties. The city's renowned beer and wine restaurants offer superb atmosphere, low prices, and as much wholesome German food as you'll ever want. They're open at just about any hour of the day or night.

## What to Wear

Many Munich restaurants serve sophisticated cuisine, and they require their patrons to dress for the occasion. Other, usually less expensive, restaurants will serve you regardless of what you wear.

| CATEGORY | COST* |
|---|---|
| $$$$ | over DM 100 |
| $$$ | DM 75–DM 100 |
| $$ | DM 50–DM 75 |
| $ | under DM 50 |

*per person for a three-course meal, including tax and excluding drinks

**$$$$  AM MARSTALL.** The latest addition to Munich's luxury restaurant scene has rapidly won acclaim—and a Michelin star. The exciting menu combines the best of French and German cuisine—lamb bred on the salt-soaked meadows of coastal Brittany, for instance, or venison from the hunting grounds of Lower Bavaria. The restaurant is on Maximilianstrasse, so if you book a window seat you can while away the time between courses by watching Bavaria's well-heeled shoppers promenading. *Maximilianstr. 16, tel. 089/ 291–6551. Reservations essential. Jacket and tie. AE, MC, V. Closed Sun., Mon., and public holidays.*

**$$$$ KÖNIGSHOF.** A Michelin star was awarded the reliable old Königshof hotel restaurant in 2000, recognition at last of its place among Munich's finest and most traditional eating places. The outstanding menu is French influenced, the surroundings elegant—and if you book a window table you'll have a view of Munich's busiest squares, the Stachus, an incandescent experience at night. *Karlspl. 25, tel. 089/5513–6142. Reservations essential. Jacket and tie. AE, DC, MC, V.*

**$$$$ TANTRIS.** Chef Hans Haas has kept this restaurant with a modernist
★ look among the top five dining establishments in Munich, and in 1994 Germany's premier food critics voted him the country's top chef. You, too, will be impressed by the exotic nouvelle cuisine on the menu, including such specialties as shellfish and creamed potato soup and roasted wood pigeon with scented rice. But you may wish to ignore the bare concrete surroundings and the garish orange-and-yellow decor. *Johann-Fichter-Str. 7, tel. 089/361–9590. Reservations essential. Jacket and tie. AE, DC, MC, V. Closed Sun.*

**$$$ BISTRO TERRINE.** Tucked away self-effacingly in a corner of a Schwabing shopping arcade, the bistro is one of this lively area's most charming upscale restaurants. Crisp blue-and-white linen, cane-back chairs, and art-nouveau lamps give it a French atmosphere matched by the excellent Gallic-influenced menu. A cozy aperitif bar completes the harmonious picture. *Amalienstr. 89, tel. 089/281–780. AE, DC, MC, V. Closed Sun. No lunch Mon.*

**$$$ DUKATZ.** ★ Join the literary crowd at this intellectuals' scene—a smart, high-vaulted bar and restaurant in the Literaturhaus, a converted city mansion where regular book readings are presented. Tables buzz with talk of publishing deals and problem authors. English-language newspapers are among the heap of reading material at your disposal in the airy café that fronts the restaurant. Food is predominantly German nouvelle cuisine, with traditional dishes such as calves' head and lamb tripe offered with a light, almost Gallic touch. *Salvatorpl. 1, tel. 089/291–9600. No credit cards.*

**$$–$$$ BISTRO CÉZANNE.** You're in for Parisian-style dining at this truly Gallic bistro-restaurant in the heart of Munich's former bohemian quarter, Schwabing. Owner-chef Patrick Geay learned his craft from some of Europe's best teachers. His regularly changing blackboard menu features the freshest market products, with vegetables prepared as only the French can. Among the fish dishes, the scallops melt in the mouth, while the coq au vin is Gallic cuisine at its most authentic. Reservations are advised. *Konradstr. 1, tel. 089/391–805. AE, MC, V.*

**$$–$$$ VINAIOLO.** Less than two years after opening in the bohemian Haidhausen district, this Italian restaurant has won a Michelin star—a record even for Munich. Despite its quick rise to fame, Vinaiolo, decorated in a restful pastel green, preserves its understated charm, and even if you order just a plate of pasta, the charming Italian staff doesn't bat a collective Mediterranean eyelid. But why stick with spaghetti when the menu is rich with such specialties as oxtail in red-wine sauce and tender wings of the giant ray fish. Reservations are advised. *Steinstr. 42, tel. 089/ 4895–0356. AE, MC, V.*

# munich dining

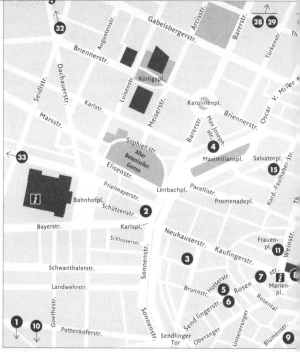

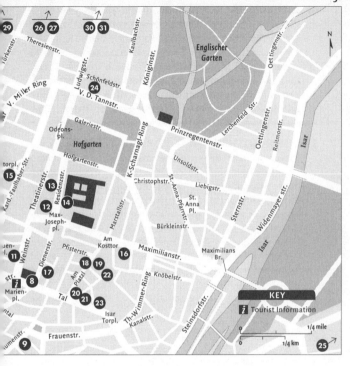

Nürnberger
Bratwurst Glöckl
am Dom, 11

Pfälzer
Weinprobier-
stube, 14

Ratskeller, 8

Spatenhaus, 12

Spöckmeier, 7

Tantris, 31

Vinaiolo, 25

Weichandhof, 32

Weinhaus
Neuner, 3

Weisses
Bräuhaus, 20

Welser Kuche, 13

Wirtshaus im
Weinstadl, 17

**$$ AUSTERNKELLER.** *Austern* (oysters) are the specialty of this cellar restaurant, although many other varieties of seafood—all flown in daily from France—help fill its imaginative menu. The lobster thermidor is expensive (DM 46) but surpasses that served elsewhere in Munich, while a rich fish soup can be had for less than DM 10. The fussy, fishnet-hung decor is a shade too maritime, especially for downtown Munich, but the starched white linen and glittering glassware and cutlery lend a note of elegance. *Stollbergstr. 11, tel. 089/298–787. AE, DC, MC, V. No lunch.*

**$$ CAFE AM BEETHOVENPLATZ.** The name of this charming café-restaurant is something of a misnomer because it's much more than a café. Beethoven is on the menu—along with countless other composers, whose piano and recital works are performed nightly on and around a grand piano that dominates one part of the large, art nouveau dining room. An international breakfast menu is served daily (on Sunday with live classic music), followed by suitably creative lunch and dinner menus. The pork is supplied by a farm where the free-range pigs are fed only the best natural fodder—so the Schweinebraten is recommended. Reservations are advised as a young and intellectual crowd fills the tables quickly. *Goethestr. 51 (am Beethovenplatz), tel. 089/5440–4348. No credit cards.*

**$$ GLOCKENBACH.** This small, highly popular restaurant with dark-wood paneling serves mostly fish entrées, prepared by the acclaimed chef and owner, Karl Ederer. Book ahead to enjoy specialties such as freshwater fish ragout from Starnberger Lake. Highlights of the meat menu are Bavarian Forest lamb and free-range chicken with wild mushrooms. *Kapuzinerstr. 29, tel. 089/ 534–043. Reservations essential. AE, MC, V. Closed Sun. and Mon.*

**$$ HALALI.** The Halali is an old-style Munich restaurant—polished wood paneling and antlers on the walls—that offers new-style regional specialties, such as venison in juniper-berry sauce and marinated beef on a bean salad. Save room for the homemade vanilla ice cream. *Schönfeldstr. 22, tel. 089/285–909. Jacket and tie. AE, MC, V. Closed Sun.*

**$$ HUNSINGERS PACIFIC.** Werner Hunsinger, one of Germany's top restaurateurs, has brought to Munich a reasonably priced restaurant serving eclectic cuisine, borrowing from the Pacific Rim of East Asia, Australia, and North and South America. The restaurant's clam chowder is the best to be found in the city, while another praised specialty is the Chilean-style fillet steak, wrapped in a mantle of onion and eggplant-flavored maize. Lunchtime two-course meals cost less than DM 20, and evening meals cost between DM 45 and DM 55. *Maximilianspl. 5, tel. 089/ 5502–9741. AE, MC, V. No lunch weekends.*

**$$ RATSKELLER.** Munich's Ratskeller under the city hall is known for its goulash soup. Seat yourself—the space is cavernous, and the setting includes vaulted stone ceilings, alcoves, banquettes, and wrought-iron work. An atmospheric tavern serves fine Franconian wine from Würzburg's famous Juliusspital at a price that can't be matched in Munich. *Marienpl. 8, tel. 089/219–9890. AE, MC, V.*

**$$ SPATENHAUS.** A view of the opera house and the royal palace ★ complements the Bavarian mood of the wood-paneled and beamed Spatenhaus. The menu is international, however, with more or less everything from artichokes to *zuppa Romana* (alcohol-soaked, fruity Italian cake-pudding). But since you're in Bavaria, why not do as the Bavarians do? Try the Bavarian plate, an enormous mixture of local meats and sausages. *Residenzstr. 12, tel. 089/290–7060. AE, MC, V.*

**$$ SPÖCKMEIER.** This rambling, solidly Bavarian beer restaurant spread over three floors, including a snug *Keller* (cellar), is famous for its homemade Weisswurst. If you've just stopped in for a snack and don't fancy the fat breakfast sausage, order coffee and pretzels or, in the afternoon, a wedge of cheesecake. The daily changing menu also offers more than two dozen hearty main-course dishes and a choice of four draft beers. The house *Eintopf* (a rich broth of noodles and pork) is a meal in itself. The Spöckmeier is only 50 yards from Marienplatz; on sunny summer days tables are set outside in the car-free street. *Rosenstr. 9, tel. 089/268–088. AE, DC, MC, V.*

**$$ WEICHANDHOF.** If you're heading to the leafy residential suburb of Obermenzing, near the start of the Stuttgart Autobahn, a stop here is strongly recommended, but even a special trip from the city center is worthwhile. The food at this old farmhouse-style restaurant is excellent, with a menu based on traditional Bavarian and regional German and Austrian fare. Roast suckling pig, pork knuckle, and Vienna-style boiled beef are staples. In summer or on warm spring and autumn evenings the vine-clad terrace beckons. In winter tiled stoves give a warm glow to the wood-paneled dining rooms. *Betzenweg 81, tel. 089/891–1600 or 089/811–1621. MC. Closed Sat.*

**$$ WEINHAUS NEUNER.** Munich's oldest wine tavern serves good food as well as superior wines in its three nooks: the wood-paneled restaurant, the Weinstübl, and the small bistro. The choice of food is remarkable, from nouvelle German to old-fashioned country. Specialties include home-smoked beef and salmon. *Herzogspitalstr. 8, tel. 089/260–3954. AE, MC, V. Closed Sun.*

**$$ WELSER KUCHE.** It's less a question of what to order at this medieval-style cellar restaurant than how you'll eat it—with your fingers and a hunting knife, in the manner of 16th-century baronial banquets. You're welcomed by pretty "serving wenches" who tie a protective bib around your neck, proffer a hunting horn of mead, and show you to one of the oak trestle tables that complete the authentic-looking surroundings. It's best to go in a group, but room will always be found for couples or those dining alone. The full menu runs to 10 dishes, although you can settle for less and choose à la carte. *Residenzstr. 2, tel. 089/296–565. MC. No lunch.*

**$$ WIRTSHAUS IM WEINSTADL.** At the end of a small alley off a busy shopping street and overlooked by most passersby, the historic 16th-century Weinstadl is well worth hunting out. In summer the courtyard beer garden is a cool delight. A fountain depicting a Munich burgher quaffing a glass of wine splashes away beneath original Renaissance galleries. In winter the brass-studded oaken door opens onto a vaulted dining room where traditional Bavarian fare is served at bench-lined tables. A lunchtime menu and a glass of excellent beer leave change from DM 20. The cellar, reached via a winding staircase, features live music on Friday and Saturday evenings. *Burgstr. 5, tel. 089/2916–1566. AE, DC, MC.*

**\$–\$\$ BAMBERGER HAUS.** The faded elegance of this historic house on the edge of Schwabing's Luitpold Park disguises an up-to-date kitchen, which conjures up inexpensive dishes of modern flair and imagination. Vegetarians are well catered to with cheap and filling vegetable gratins. The cellar beer tavern serves one of the best ales in town. In summer reserve a table on the terrace and eat under chestnut trees with a view of the park. *Brunnerstr. 2, tel. 089/308–8966. AE, DC, MC, V.*

**\$ AUGUSTINER KELLER.** This 19th-century establishment is the flagship beer restaurant of one of Munich's oldest breweries, Augustiner. The decor emphasizes wood—from the refurbished parquet floors to the wood barrels from which the beer is drawn. The menu changes daily and offers a full range of Bavarian specialties, but try to order Tellerfleisch, served on a big wooden board. Follow that with *Dampfnudeln* (suet pudding served with custard), and you won't feel hungry again for 24 hours. The communal atmosphere of the two baronial hall-like rooms makes this a better place for meeting locals than for a quiet meal for two. *Arnulfstr. 52, tel. 089/594–393. AE, MC, V.*

**\$ BRAUHAUS ZUM BREZ'N.** This hostelry is bedecked in the blue-and-white-check colors of the Bavarian flag. The eating and drinking are spread over three floors and cater to a broad clientele—from local business lunchers to hungry night owls emerging from Schwabing's bars and looking for a bite at 2 AM.

Brez'n offers a big all-day menu of traditional roasts, to be washed down with a choice of three draft beers. *Leopoldstr. 72, tel. 089/390–092. AE, DC, MC, V.*

**$ DÜRNBRÄU.** A fountain plays outside this picturesque old Bavarian inn. Inside, it's crowded and noisy. Expect to share a table; your fellow diners will range from businesspeople to students. The food is resolutely traditional. Try the cream of spinach soup and the boiled beef. *Dürnbräug. 2, tel. 089/222–195. AE, DC, MC, V.*

**$ ERSTES MÜNCHNER KARTOFFELHAUS.** In Munich's First Potato House tubers come in all forms, from the simplest baked potato with sour cream to gratin creations with shrimp and salmon. When potatoes were first introduced to Germany, they were dismissed as fodder fit only for animals or the very lowest strata of society. Frederick the Great was largely responsible for putting them on the dining tables of even the nobility, and now the lowly potato is an indispensable part of the German diet. This restaurant is great fun and a great value, too. *Hochbrückenstr. 3, tel. 089/296–331. Reservations essential. AE, MC.*

**$ GRÜNE GANS.** This small, chummy restaurant near the Viktualienmarkt is popular with local entertainers, whose photos clutter the walls. International fare with regional German influences dominates the menu, and there are a few Chinese dishes. Try the chervil cream soup, followed by calves' kidneys in tarragon sauce. *Am Einlass 5, tel. 089/266–228. Reservations essential. No credit cards. Closed Sun.*

**$ HACKERHAUS.** Since the 15th century, beer has been brewed or served here, the birthplace of Hacker-Pschorr, a still-active Munich brewery. Today the site is a cozy, upscale restaurant with three floors of wood-paneled rooms. In summer you can order a cheese plate and beer in the cool, flower-decorated inner courtyard; in winter you can snuggle in a corner of the Ratsstube and warm up on thick homemade potato broth, followed by schnitzel and *Bratkartoffein* (panfried potatoes), or take a table in the Bürgerstube and admire its proud centerpiece, the world's largest beer mug. *Sendlingerstr. 14, tel. 089/260–5026. AE, DC, MC, V.*

$ **HAXENBAUER.** This is one of Munich's more sophisticated beer restaurants. There's the usual series of interlinking rooms and sturdy yet pretty Bavarian decoration. But there is a much greater emphasis on the food here than in similar places. Try the *Schweineshaxn* (pork shanks) cooked over a charcoal fire. *Münzstr. 2, tel. 089/2916–2100. AE, MC, V.*

$ **HOFBRÄUHAUS.** The pounding oompah band draws passersby into this father of all beer halls, where singing and shouting drinkers contribute to the earsplitting din. This is no place for the fainthearted, although a trip to Munich would be incomplete without a look in. Upstairs is a quieter restaurant. In March, May, and September ask for one of the special, extra-strong seasonal beers (Starkbier, Maibock, Märzen), which complement the heavy, traditional Bavarian fare. *Am Platzl 9, tel. 089/221–676 or 089/290–1360. Reservations not accepted. V.*

$ **HUNDSKUGEL.** This is Munich's oldest tavern and also one of the
★ city's smallest. You'll be asked to squeeze up and make room for latecomers looking for a place at one of the few tables that clutter the handkerchief-size dining room. The tavern dates from 1440 and in many ways doesn't appear to have changed much over the centuries. Even the menu is medievally basic and a bit hit-and-miss, although any combination of pork and potato or sauerkraut can be recommended. *Hotterstr. 18, tel. 089/264–272. No credit cards.*

$ **MAX-EMANUEL-BRAUEREI.** This historic old brewery tavern is a great value, with Bavarian dishes rarely costing more than DM 20; at lunchtime that amount will easily cover the cost of an all-you-can-eat buffet including a couple of beers. The main dining room has a stage, so the bill often includes a cabaret or jazz concert. In summer take a table outside in the secluded little beer garden. *Adalbertstr. 33, tel. 089/271–5158. AE, MC.*

# Eating Well is the Best Revenge

Eating out is a major part of every travel experience. It's a chance to explore flavors you don't find at home. And often the walking you do on vacation means that you can dig in without guilt.

**START AT THE TOP** By all means take in a really good restaurant or two while you're on the road. A trip is a time to kick back and savor the pleasures of the palate. Read up on the culinary scene before you leave home. Check out representative menus on the Web—some chefs have gone electronic. And ask friends who have just come back. Then reserve a table as far in advance as you can, remembering that the best establishments book up months in advance. Remember that some good restaurants require you to reconfirm the day before or the day of your meal. Then again, some really good places will call you, so make sure to leave a number where you can be reached.

**ADVENTURES IN EATING** A trip is the perfect opportunity to try food you can't get at home. So leave yourself open to try an ethnic food that's not represented where you live or to eat fruits and vegetables you've never heard of. One of them may become your next favorite food.

**BEYOND GUIDEBOOKS** You can rely on the restaurants you find in these pages. But also look for restaurants on your own. When you're ready for lunch, ask people you meet where they eat. Look for tiny holes-in-the-wall with a loyal following and the best burgers or crispiest pizza crust. Find out about local chains whose fame rests upon a single memorable dish. There's hardly a food-lover who doesn't relish the chance to share a favorite place. It's fun to come up with your own special find—and asking about food is a great way to start a conversation.

**SAMPLE LOCAL FLAVORS** Do check out the specialties. Is there a special brand of ice cream or a special dish that you simply must try?

**HAVE A PICNIC** Every so often eat al fresco. Grocery shopping gives you a whole different view of a place.

**$ NÜRNBERGER BRATWURST GLÖCKL AM DOM.** Munich's most original beer tavern is dedicated to a specialty from a rival city, Nuremberg, whose delicious *Nürnberger Bratwürste* (finger-size sausages) form the staple dish of the menu. They're served by a busy team of friendly waitresses dressed in Bavarian dirndls, who flit between the crowded tables with remarkable agility. In summer tables are placed outside under a bright awning and in the shade of the nearby Frauenkirche. In winter the mellow dark-paneled dining rooms provide relief from the cold. *Frauenpl. 9, tel. 089/220–385. No credit cards.*

**$ PFÄLZER WEINPROBIERSTUBE.** A warren of stone-vaulted rooms, wooden tables, flickering candles, dirndl-clad waitresses, and a vast range of wines add up to an experience as close to everyone's image of timeless Germany as you're likely to get. The wines are mostly from the *Pfalz* (Palatinate), as are many of the specialties on the limited menu. Here you'll find former chancellor Kohl's favorite dish, *Saumagen* (meat loaf, spiced with herbs and cooked in a pig's stomach). *Residenzstr. 1, tel. 089/225–628. Reservations not accepted. No credit cards.*

**$ WEISSES BRÄUHAUS.** If you have developed a taste for Munich's Weissbier, this is the place to enjoy it. Other beers, including a very strong Aventinus, are available, but the accent is unmistakably on the Schneider brewery's famous specialty, the Schneiderweisse, a yeast-fermented wheat beer. It's served with hearty Bavarian dishes, mostly variations of pork and dumplings or cabbage, by some of Munich's friendliest waitresses, good-humored women in crisp black dresses, who appear to match the Jugendstil features of the restaurant's beautifully restored interior. *Tal 7, tel. 089/299–875. No credit cards.*

## In This Section

# shopping

## Shopping Districts

Munich has an immense central shopping area, a 2-km (1-mi) Fussgängerzone (pedestrian zone) stretching from the train station to Marienplatz and north to Odeonsplatz. The two main streets here are Neuhauserstrasse and Kaufingerstrasse, the sites of most major department stores. For upscale shopping, Maximilianstrasse, Residenzstrasse, and Theatinerstrasse are unbeatable and contain a fine array of classy and tempting stores that are the equal of any in Europe. Schwabing, north of the university, has several of the city's most intriguing and offbeat shopping streets—Schellingstrasse and Hohenzollernstrasse are two to try.

## Antiques

Bavarian antiques—from a chipped pottery beer mug to a massive farmhouse dresser—can be found in the many small shops around the Viktualienmarkt, including on Westenriederstrasse, just south of the market. Also try the area north of the university; Türkenstrasse, Theresienstrasse, and Barerstrasse are all filled with antiques stores.

In **Antike Uhren Eder** (Prannerstr. 4, in the Hotel Bayerischer Hof building, tel. 089/220–305), the silence is broken only by the ticking of dozens of highly valuable German antique clocks and by discreet bargaining over the high prices. The nearby **Antike Uhren H. Schley** (Kardinal-Faulhaber-Str. 14a, tel. 089/226–188) also specializes in antique clocks. **Roman Odesser**

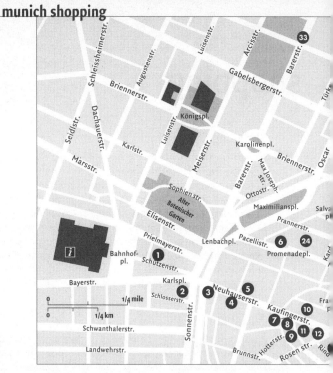

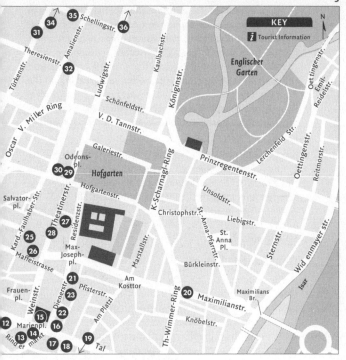

KEY

*i* Tourist Information

Englischer Garten

(Westenriederstr. 16, tel. 089/226–388) specializes in German antique silver and porcelain. Also on Westenriederstrasse, at Number 8, is a building that houses three antiques shops packed from floor to ceiling with curios, including a great collection of ancient dolls and toys. For Munich's largest selection of dolls and marionettes, travel to Schwabing, to **Die Puppenstube** (Luisenstr. 68, tel. 089/272–3267). For nautical items or ancient sports equipment (golf clubs, for instance) try the **Captain's Saloon** (Westenriederstr. 31, tel. 089/221–015).

Strictly for window-shopping—unless you're looking for something really rare and special, and money's no object—are the exclusive shops lining Prannerstrasse, at the rear of the Hotel Bayerischer Hof. Interesting and/or cheap antiques and assorted junk from all over eastern Europe are laid out at the weekend **flea markets** beneath the Donnersberger railway bridge on Arnulfstrasse (along the northern side of the Hauptbahnhof).

## Department Stores

**Hertie** (Bahnhofpl. 7, tel. 089/55120), occupying an entire city block between the train station and Karlsplatz, is the largest and, some claim, the best department store in the city. The basement has a high-class delicatessen with champagne bar and a stand-up bistro offering a daily changing menu that puts many high-price Munich restaurants to shame. Hertie's Schwabing branch (tel. 089/381–060) is the high-gloss steel-and-glass building on the square known as Münchner-Freiheit. **Karstadt** (Neuhauserstr. 18, tel. 089/290–230), in the 100-year-old Haus Oberpollinger, at the start of the Kaufingerstrasse shopping mall, is another upscale department store, with a very wide range of Bavarian arts and crafts. Karstadt also has a Schwabing branch, **Karstadt am Nordbad** (Schleissheimerstr. 93, tel. 089/13020). **Kaufhof**'s two central Munich stores (Karlspl. 21–24, tel. 089/51250; Corner Kaufingerstr. and Marienpl., tel. 089/231–851) offer a range of goods in the middle price range. If you catch an end-of-season sale, you're sure to get a bargain.

**Ludwig Beck** (Marienpl. 11, tel. 089/236–910) is considered a step above other departments stores by Müncheners. It's packed from top to bottom with highly original wares—from fine feather boas to roughly finished Bavarian pottery. In December a series of booths, each delicately and lovingly decorated, is occupied by craftspeople turning out traditional German toys and decorations. **Hirmer** (Kaufingerstr. 28, tel. 089/236–830) has Munich's most comprehensive collection of German-made men's clothes, with a markedly friendly and knowledgeable staff. **K & L Ruppert** (Kaufingerstr. 15, tel. 089/ 231–1470) has a fashionable range of German-made clothes in the lower price brackets.

## Folk Costumes

If you want to deck yourself out in lederhosen or a dirndl or affect a green loden coat and little pointed hat with feathers, you have a wide choice in the Bavarian capital. Much of the fine loden clothing on sale at **Lodenfrey** (Maffeistr. 7–9, tel. 089/210–390) is made at the company's own factory, on the edge of the Englischer Garten. **Wallach** (Residenzstr. 3, tel. 089/220–871) has souvenirs downstairs and shoes and clothing upstairs (though no children's wear). The tiny **Lederhosen Wagner** (Tal 2, tel. 089/225–697) carries lederhosen, woolen sweaters called *Walk* (not loden), and children's clothing.

## Food Markets

Munich's **Viktualienmarkt** is the place to shop. Just south of Marienplatz, it's home to an array of colorful stands that sell everything from cheese to sausages, from flowers to wine. A visit here is more than just collecting picnic makings; it's central to an understanding of the Müncheners' easy-come-easy-go nature. If you're in the Schwabing area, the daily market at **Elisabethplatz** is worth a visit—it's much, much smaller than the Viktualienmarkt, but the range and quality of produce are comparable.

**Dallmayr** (Dienerstr. 14–15, tel. 089/21350) is an elegant gourmet food store, with delights ranging from the most exotic fruits to English jams, served by efficient Munich matrons in smart blue-and-white-linen costumes. The store's famous specialty is coffee, with more than 50 varieties to blend as you wish. There's also an enormous range of breads and a temperature-controlled cigar room.

The **Zerwick Gewölbe** (Ledererstr. 3, tel. 089/226–824) is Munich's oldest venison shop, with a mouthwatering selection of smoked meats, including wild boar.

## Gift Ideas

Munich is a city of beer, and items related to its consumption are obvious choices for souvenirs and gifts. Visit **Ludwig Mory** (Marienpl. 8, tel. 089/224–542), **Wilhelm Müller** (Sendlingerstr. 34, tel. 089/263–969), or **Sebastian Wesely** (Rindermarkt 1 [am Peterspl.], tel. 089/264–519).

Munich is also the home of the famous **Nymphenburg Porcelain** factory. The **Nymphenburg store** (Corner of Odeonspl. and Briennerstr., tel. 089/282–428) resembles a drawing room of the famous Munich palace, with dove-gray soft furnishings and the delicate, expensive porcelain safely locked away in bowfront cabinets. You can also buy direct from the factory, on the grounds of **Schloss Nymphenburg** (Nördliches Schlossrondell 8, tel. 089/1791–9710). For Dresden and Meissen ware, go to **Kunstring Meissen** (Briennerstr. 4, tel. 089/281–532).

Bavarian craftspeople have a showplace of their own, the **Bayerischer Kunstgewerbe–Verein** (Pacellistr. 6–8, tel. 089/290–1470); here you'll find every kind of handicraft, from glass and pottery to textiles.

**Otto Kellnberger's Holzhandlung** (Heiliggeiststr. 7–8, tel. 089/ 226–479) specializes in wooden crafts. Looking for that pig's-bristle brush to get to the bottom of tall champagne glasses? **Geschenk Alm** (Heiliggeiststr. 7–8, tel. 089/226–479) has nooks and crannies filled with brushes of every kind.

**Obletter's** (Karlspl. 11–12, tel. 089/5508–9510) has two extensive floors of toys, many of them handmade playthings of great charm and quality. From November's end until December 24, the open-air stalls of the **Christkindlmarkt** (Marienpl.) are a great place to find gifts and warm up with mulled wine. Two other perennial Christmas market favorites are those in Schwabing (Münchner-Freiheit Square) and at the Chinesischer Turm, in the middle of the Englischer Garten.

## Malls

The main pedestrian area has two malls. **Kaufinger Tor** (Kaufingerstr. 117) has several floors of boutiques and cafés packed neatly together under a high glass roof. The aptly named **Arcade** (Neuhauserstr. 5) is where the young find the best designer jeans and chunky jewelry.

## In This Section

# outdoor activities and sports

THE OLYMPIAPARK (☞ Outside the Center in Here and There), built for the 1972 Olympics, is one of the largest sports and recreation centers in Europe. For general information about sports opportunities in and around Munich contact the sports emporium Sport Scheck (Sendlingerstr. 6, tel. 089/21660). The big store not only sells every kind of equipment but is very handy with advice.

## Beaches and Water Sports

There is sailing and windsurfing on both the Ammersee and the Starnbergersee (☞ Side Trips). Windsurfers should pay attention to restricted areas at bathing beaches. Information on sailing is available from **Bayerischer Segler-Verband** (Georg-Brauchle-Ring 93, tel. 089/1570–2366). For information on windsurfing contact **Verband der Deutschen Windsurfing Schulen** (Weilheim, tel. 0881/5267).

## Golf

The **Munich Golf Club** has two courses that admit visitors on weekdays. Visitors must be members of a club at home. Its 18-hole course is at Strasslach in the suburb of Grünwald, south of the city (tel. 08170/450). The greens fee is DM 120. Its nine-hole course is more centrally located, at **Thalkirchen**, on the Isar River (tel. 089/723–1304). The greens fee starts at DM 80, depending on the number of holes played.

## Ice-Skating

The **Eissportstadion** in Olympiapark (Spiridon-Louis-Ring 3) has an indoor rink, and outdoor rinks are available at **Prinzregenten Stadium** (Prinzregentenstr. 80) and **Eisbahn-West** (Agnes-Bernauer Str. 241). Depending on weather conditions, there's also outdoor skating in winter on the lake in the **Englischer Garten** and on the **Nymphenburger Canal**, where you can also go curling (*Eisstockschiessen*) by renting equipment from little wooden huts, which also sell hot drinks. Players rent sections of machine-smoothed ice on the canal. Watch out for signs reading GEFAHR (danger), warning you of thin ice. Additional information is available from **Bayerischer Eissportverband** (Georg-Brauchle-Ring 93, tel. 089/157–9920).

## Jogging

The best place to jog is the **Englischer Garten** (U-bahn: Münchner-Freiheit or Universität), which is 11 km (7 mi) around and has lakes and dirt and asphalt paths. You can also jog through **Olympiapark** (U-bahn: Olympiazentrum). The 500-acre park of **Schloss Nymphenburg** and the banks of the **Isar River** are also ideal for running. For a longer jog along the river, take the S-bahn to Unterföhring and pace yourself back to Münchner-Freiheit—a distance of 6½ km (4 mi).

## Rowing

Rowboats can be rented on the south shore of the **Olympiasee** in Olympiapark and at the **Kleinhesseloher See** in the Englischer Garten.

## Swimming

You can try swimming outdoors in the Isar River at Maria-Einsiedel, but because the river flows down from the Alps, the water is frigid even in summer. Warmer lakes near Munich are the **Ammersee** and the **Starnbergersee** (☞ Side Trips). There are pools at the **Cosima Bad** (Englschalkingerstr. and Cosimastr., Bogenhausen), with man-made waves; the **Dantebad** (Dantestr. 6), **Nordbad** (Schleissheimerstr. 142, in Schwabing district), and the **Michaelibad** (Heinrich-Wieland-Str. 24) have indoor and outdoor pools; the **Olympia-Schwimmhalle** (Olympiapark) and the **Müllersches Volksbad** (Rosenheimerstr. 1) have indoor pools.

## Tennis

There are indoor and outdoor courts at **Münchnerstrasse 15,** in München-Unterföhring; at the corner of **Drygalski-Allee** and **Kistlerhofstrasse,** in München-Fürstenried; and at **Rothof Sportanlage** (Denningerstr., behind the Arabella and Sheraton hotels). In addition, there are about 200 outdoor courts all over Munich. Many can be booked via the sports store **Sport Scheck** (tel. 089/21660), which has branches around town. Prices vary from DM 18 to DM 25 an hour, depending on the time of day. Full details on tennis in Munich are available from the **Bayerischer Tennis Verband** (Georg-Brauchle-Ring 93, tel. 089/157–030).

## In This Section

# nightlife and the arts

## THE ARTS

Bavaria's capital has an enviable reputation as an artistic hot spot. Details of concerts and theater performances are listed in "Vorschau" and "Monatsprogramm," booklets available at most hotel reception desks, newsstands, and tourist offices. Some hotels will make ticket reservations, or you can book through ticket agencies in the city center, such as Max Hieber Konzertkasse (Liebfrauenstr. 1, tel. 089/2900–8014), the two Zentraler Kartenverkauf kiosks in the underground concourse at Marienplatz (tel. 089/264–620), the Abendzeitung Schalterhalle (Sendlingerstr. 10, tel. 089/267–024), or Residenz Bücherstube (concert tickets only; Residenzstr. 1, tel. 089/220–868). Tickets for performances at the Altes Residenztheater/Cuvilliés-Theater, Bavarian State Theater/New Residence Theater, Nationaltheater, Prinzregententheater, and Staatheater am Gartnerplatz are sold at the central box office (Maximilianstr. 11, tel. 089/2185–1920). It's open weekdays 10–6, Saturday 10–1, and one hour before curtain time. One ticket agency, München Ticket (tel. 089/5481–8181, www.muenchenticket.de) has a German-language Web site where tickets for most Munich theaters can be booked.

## Concerts

Munich and music go together. Its world-class concert hall, the **Gasteig Culture Center** (Rosenheimerstr. 5, tel. 089/5481–8181), is a lavish brick complex standing high above the Isar River, east of downtown. Its Philharmonic Hall is the permanent home of the Munich Philharmonic Orchestra. The city has three other principal orchestras, and the leading choral ensembles are the Munich Bach Choir, the Munich Motettenchor, and Musica Viva—the latter specializing in contemporary music. The choirs perform mostly in city churches.

The Bavarian Radio Symphony Orchestra performs at the **Bayerischer Rundfunk** (Rundfunkpl. 1, tel. 089/558–080) and also at other city venues. The box office is open Monday–Thursday 9–noon and 2–4, Friday 9–noon.

The Bavarian State Orchestra is based at the **Nationaltheater** (also called the Bayerische Staatsoper; Opernpl., tel. 089/2185–1920). The Kurt Graunke Symphony Orchestra performs at the romantic Art-Nouveau **Staatstheater am Gärtnerplatz** (Gärtnerpl. 3, tel. 089/201–6767).

**Herkulessaal in der Residenz** (Hofgarten, tel. 089/2906–7263) is a leading orchestral and recital venue. Concerts featuring conservatory students are given free of charge at the **Hochschule für Musik** (Arcisstr. 12, tel. 089/128–901).

Munich's major pop/rock concert venue is the **Olympiahalle** (tel. 089/3061–3577). The box office, at the ice stadium, is open weekdays 10–6 and Saturday 10–3. You can also book by calling **München Ticket** (tel. 089/5481–8181).

## Opera, Ballet, and Musicals

Munich's Bavarian State Opera Company and its ballet ensemble perform at the **Nationaltheater** (☞ *above*). The **Staatstheater am Gärtnerplatz** (☞ *above*) presents a less ambitious but nevertheless high-quality program of opera, ballet, operetta, and musicals.

## Theater

Munich has scores of theaters and variety-show venues, although most productions will be largely impenetrable if your

German is shaky. Listed here are all the better-known theaters, as well as some of the smaller and more progressive spots. Note that most theaters are closed during July and August.

**Altes Residenztheater/Cuvilliés-Theater** (Max-Joseph-Pl.; entrance on Residenzstr., tel. 089/2185–1920). This is an intimate stage for compact opera productions such as Mozart's *Singspiele* and classic and contemporary plays (Arthur Miller met with great success here).

**Amerika Haus** (America House; Karolinenpl. 3, tel. 089/343–803). A very active American company, the American Drama Group Europe, presents regular productions here.

**Bayerisches Staatsschauspiel/Neues Residenztheater** (Bavarian State Theater/New Residence Theater; Max-Joseph-Pl., tel. 089/2185–1940). This is Munich's leading stage for classic playwrights such as Goethe, Schiller, Lessing, Shakespeare, and Chekhov.

**Deutsches Theater** (Schwanthalerstr. 13, tel. 089/5523–4444). Musicals, revues, and big-band shows take place here. The box office is open weekdays noon–6, Saturday 10–1:30.

**Feierwerk** (Hansastr. 39, tel. 089/769–3600). English-language productions are regularly presented at this venue.

The Carl-Orff Saal and the Black Box theaters, in the **Gasteig Culture Center** (☞ *above*), occasionally present English-language plays. The box office is open weekdays 10:30–6, Saturday 10–2.

**Komödie im Bayerischen Hof** (Bayerischer Hof Hotel, Promenadenpl., tel. 089/292–810) and **Kleine Komödie am Max II** (Max-II-Denkmal, Maximilianstr. 47, tel. 089/221–859) share a program of light comedy and farce. The box office at Bayerischer Hof is open Monday–Saturday 11–8, Sunday 3–8. The box office at Max-II-Denkmal is open Monday–Saturday 11–8, Sunday 2–6.

**Münchner Kammerspiele-Schauspielhaus** (Maximilianstr. 26, tel. 089/2333–7000). A city-funded rival to the nearby state-backed Staatliches Schauspiel, this theater of international renown presents the classics and new works by contemporary playwrights.

**Prinzregententheater** (Prinzregentenpl. 12, tel. 089/2185–2959). Munich's Art-Nouveau theater, an audience favorite, presents not only opera but musicals and musical gala events.

Munich also has several theaters for children. With pantomime such a strong part of the repertoire, the language problem disappears. The best of these theaters are the **Münchner Theater für Kinder** (Dachauerstr. 46, tel. 089/595–454) and the **Schauburg Theater der Jugend** (Franz-Joseph-Str. 47, tel. 089/2333–7171). Three puppet theaters offer regular performances: the **Münchner Marionettentheater** (Blumenstr. 32, tel. 089/265–712), the **Marionettenbühne Zaubergarten** (Nikolaistr. 17, tel. 089/271–3373), and **Otto Bille's Marionettenbühne** (Breiterangerstr. 15, tel. 089/150–2168). Munich is the winter quarters of the big-top **Circus Krone** (Marsstr. 43, tel. 089/558–166), which performs from Christmas until the end of March.

# NIGHTLIFE

Munich's nocturnal attractions vary with the seasons. The year starts with the abandon of Fasching, the Bavarian carnival time, which begins quietly in mid-November with the crowning of the King and Queen of Fools, expands with fancy-dress balls, and ends with a great street party on Fasching Dienstag (Shrove Tuesday) in early March. Men should forget wearing neckties on Fasching Dienstag: women posing as witches make it a point of cutting them off. From spring until late fall the beer garden dictates the style and pace of Munich's nightlife. When it rains, the indoor beer halls and taverns absorb the thirsty like blotting paper.

The beer gardens and most beer halls close at midnight, but there's no need to go home to bed: some bars and nightclubs are open until 6 AM. A word of caution about some of those bars: most are run honestly, and prices are only slightly higher than normal, but a few may intentionally overcharge. The seedier ones are near the main train station. Stick to beer or wine if you can, and pay as you go. And if you feel you're being duped, call the cops—the customer is usually, if not always, right.

## Bars

Every Munich bar is singles territory. Wait until after midnight before venturing into the **Alter Simpl** (Türkenstr. 57, tel. 089/272–3083), where a sparkling crowd enlivens the gloomy surroundings. Munich's latest "in" haunt resides within a sleek glass-and-steel interior. **Eisbach** (Marstallstr. 2, tel. 089/2280–1680) occupies a corner of the Max Planck Institute building opposite the Bavarian Parliament. The bar is among Munich's longest and is overlooked by a mezzanine restaurant area where you can choose from a limited but ambitious menu. Outdoor tables nestle in the expansive shade of huge parasols. The nearby Eisbach Brook, which gives the bar its name, tinkles away like ice in the glass.

**Havana** (Herrnstr. 3, tel. 089/291–884) does its darndest to look like a rundown Cuban dive, but the chic clientele spoils those pretensions. The Bayerischer Hof's **Night Club** (Promenadepl. 2–6, tel. 089/212–0994) has live music, a small dance floor, and a very lively bar (avoid the poorly made mixed drinks). Jazz groups perform regularly there, too. On fashionable Maximilianstrasse, **O'Reilly's Irish Cellar Pub** (Maximilianstr. 29, tel. 089/293–311) offers escape from the German bar scene as it pours genuine Irish Guinness. Great Caribbean cocktails and Irish-German black and tans (Guinness and strong German beer) are made to the sounds of live jazz at the English nautical-style **Pusser's** bar (Falkenturmstr. 9, tel. 089/220–500).

Watch the barmen shake those cocktails at **Schumann's** (Maximilianstr. 36, tel. 089/229–060) anytime after the curtain comes down at the nearby opera house (the bar is closed on Saturday). Exotic cocktails are also the specialty of **Trader Vic's** (Promenadenpl. 2–6, tel. 089/212–0995), a smart cellar bar in the Hotel Bayerischer Hof. The bar is particularly popular among out-of-town visitors and attracts quite a few Americans. The **Vier Jahreszeiten Kempinski** (Maximilianstr. 17, tel. 089/21250) offers piano music until 9 and then dancing to recorded music or a small combo.

Munich's gay scene stretches between Sendlingertorplatz and Isartorplatz. Its most popular bars are **Nil** (Hans-Sachs-Str. 2, tel. 089/265–545), **Sax** (Hans-Sachs-Str. 3, tel. 089/265–493), **Ochsengarten** (Müllerstr. 47, tel. 089/266–446), and **Mrs. Henderson** (Müllerstr. 1, tel. 089/263–469), which also puts on the city's best transvestite cabaret for a mixed crowd.

## Dance Clubs

Schwabing is discoland, although it's getting ever greater competition from Munich's other "in" area, Haidhausen. A former Haidhausen factory hosts the city's largest rave scene: the **Kunstpark Ost** (Grafingerstr. 6, S-bahn, bus, and tram stops are at Ostbahnhof, tel. 089/490–02928). The venue has no fewer than 17 "entertainment areas," including a Latin dance club among others, bars, and a huge slot-machine and computer-game hall. Schwabing claims more than a dozen dance clubs and live music venues between its central boulevard Leopoldstrasse and the area around its central square, the Münchner-Freiheit. One, the **Skyline** (tel. 089/333–131), is at the top of the Hertie department store, which towers above the busy square. Around the corner, two streets—Feilitzstrasse and Occamstrasse—are lined with clubs, discos, and pubs. Bordering the English Garden, **PI** (Prinzregentenstr., on west side of Haus der Kunst, tel. 089/294–252) is the trendiest club in town; good luck making it past the bouncer. **Maximilian's**

**Nightclub** (Maximilianpl. 16, tel. 089/223–252), and the **Park-Café** (Sophienstr. 7, tel. 089/598–313) are similarly fashionable places where you'll have to talk yourself past the doorman to join the chic crowds inside.

**Nachtwerk** (Landsbergerstr. 185, tel. 089/570–7390), in a converted factory, blasts out a range of sounds from punk to avant-garde nightly between 8 PM and 4 AM. Live bands also perform there regularly. The real ravers ride the S-bahn to Munich's Franz-Josef-Strauss Airport, alighting at the Besucherpark station for techno and other beats until dawn at **Night Flight** (tel. 089/9759–7999). It's becoming fashionable for package-tour travelers to start their holidays here with a pre-check-in, early morning turn around the dance floor, and a bar breakfast.

## Jazz

Munich likes to think it's Germany's jazz capital, and some beer gardens have taken to replacing their brass bands with funky combos. Purists don't like it, but jazz enthusiasts are happy. Some city pubs and brewery taverns set aside Sunday midday for jazz. The best of the jazz clubs are **Mr. B's** (Herzog-Heinrich-Str. 38, tel. 089/534–901), run by New Yorker Alex Best, who also mixes great cocktails; **Jazzclub Unterfahrt im Einstein** (Einsteinstr. 42, tel. 089/448–2794); **Nachtcafé** (Maximilianpl. 5, tel. 089/595–900); and **Schwabinger Podium** (Wagnerstr. 1, tel. 089/399–482). Sunday is also set aside for jazz at **Waldwirtschaft Grosshesselohe** (Georg-Kalb-Str. 3, tel. 089/795–088), in the southern suburb of Grosshesselohe. If it's a nice day, the excursion is worth it.

## In This Section

# side trips

MUNICH'S EXCELLENT SUBURBAN RAILWAY NETWORK, the S-bahn, brings several quaint towns and attractive rural areas within easy reach for a day's excursion. The two nearest lakes, the Starnbergersee and the Ammersee, are highly recommended year-round. Dachau attracts overseas visitors, mostly because of its concentration-camp memorial site, but it's a picturesque and historic town in its own right. Landshut, north of Munich, is way off the tourist track, but if it were the same distance south of Munich, this jewel of a Bavarian market town would be overrun. Wasserburg am Inn is held in the narrow embrace of the Inn River. All these destinations have a wide selection of restaurants and hotels, and you can bring a bike on any S-bahn train.

## STARNBERGERSEE

*20 km (12 mi) southwest of Munich.*

The Starnbergersee was one of Europe's first pleasure grounds. Royal coaches were already trundling out from Munich to the lake's wooded shores in the 17th century; in 1663 Elector Ferdinand Maria threw a shipboard party at which 500 guests wined and dined as 100 oarsmen propelled them around the lake. Today pleasure steamers provide a taste of such luxury to the masses. The lake is still lined with the baroque palaces of Bavaria's aristocracy, but their owners now share the lakeside with public parks, beaches, and boatyards. The Starnbergersee is one of Bavaria's largest lakes—19 km (12 mi) long and 5 km (3 mi) wide—so there's plenty of room for swimmers, sailors, and windsurfers. On its west shore is a great golf course, but it's about as difficult to gain entrance there as it was for a commoner to attend one of Prince Ferdinand's boating parties.

## Exploring Starnbergersee

The Starnbergersee is named after its chief resort, **Starnberg,** the largest town on the lake and the nearest to Munich. Pleasure boats set off from Starnberg's jetty for trips around the lake. The resort has a tree-lined lakeside promenade and some fine turn-of-the-century villas, some of which are now hotels. There are abundant restaurants, taverns, and chestnut-tree-shaded beer gardens. On the lake's eastern shore at the village of Berg you'll find the **King Ludwig II Memorial Chapel.** A well-marked path leads through thick woods to the chapel, built near the point in the lake where the drowned king's body was found on June 13, 1886. He had been confined in nearby Berg Castle after the Bavarian government took action against his withdrawal from reality and his bankrupting castle-building fantasies. Look for the cross in the lake, which marks the point where his body was recovered.

The castle of **Possenhofen,** home of Ludwig's favorite cousin, Sisi, stands on the western shore, practically opposite Berg. Local lore says they used to send affectionate messages across the lake to each other. Sisi married the Austrian emperor Franz Joseph I but spent more than 20 summers in the lakeside castle, now a luxury hotel, the **Kaiserin Elisabeth**. Tutzingerstr. 2–6, D–82340 Feldafing, tel. 08157/1013.

Just offshore is the tiny **Roseninsel** (Rose Island), where King Maximilian II built a summer villa. You can swim to its tree-fringed shores or sail across in a dinghy or on a Windsurfer (Possenhofen's boatyard is one of the lake's many rental points).

# Eating Out and Where to Stay

**$$$  FORSTHAUS AM SEE.** The handsome, geranium-covered Forsthaus faces the lake, and so do most of the rooms (they're more expensive than those at the back with woodland views but worth it). The pinewood-furnished rooms are large, many with sitting areas. The excellent restaurant has a daily-changing international menu, with lake fish a specialty. The hotel has its own lake access and boat pier, with a chestnut-shaded beer garden nearby. *Am See 1, D–82343 Possenhofen, tel. 08157/93010, fax 08157/4292. 20 rooms, 1 suite. Restaurant, beer garden. AE, MC, V.*

**$$–$$$$  HOTEL SCHLOSS BERG.** King Ludwig II spent his final days in the small castle of Berg, from which this comfortable hotel gets its name. It's on the edge of the castle park where Ludwig liked to walk and a stone's throw from the lake shallows where he drowned. The older, century-old main hotel building is on the lakeside, while a modern annex overlooks the lake from the woods. All rooms are spacious and furnished in an elegant variation of farmhouse style. The restaurant and waterside beer garden are favorite haunts of locals and weekenders. *Seestr. 17, D–82335 Berg, tel. 08151/9630, fax 08151/96352. 50 rooms. Restaurant, bar, beer garden, sauna, bicycles. AE, MC, V. www.hotelschlossberg.de*

**$$  FORSTHAUS ILKA-HÖHE.** This fine old country lodge is set amid meadows above the lake, an uphill stroll from the Tutzing station at the end of the S-6 suburban line. The walk is well worth the effort, for the Ilka-Höhe is one of the region's most attractive restaurants, with a view of the lake. In summer dine on its vine-clad terrace. Reservations are advised, but dress is casual. *Auf der Ilkehöhe, Tutzing, tel. 08158/8242. MC. Closed Mon. and Tues., last 2 wks Dec., and weekends Jan.*

**$$  SEERESTAURANT UNDOSA.** This lakeside restaurant is only a short walk from the Starnberg railroad station and boat pier. Most tables command a view of the lake, which provides some of the

Dachau

A92

TO LANDSHUT

A99

München

Otto-brunn

Kirchseeon

Eber

Grafi

A96

Unterhaching

Stegen

Inning

Pullach

Taufkchn

Hohenbrunn

Grünwald

Oberhaching

Feldkirchen

Starnberg

Herrsching

Ammersee

Berg

13

Westerhan

Wolfratshausen

Bruc

Diessen

Tutzing

Geretsried

Holzkirchen

Starnbergersee

Isar

A95

Bad Tölz

Gmund

472

Schlierse

TO LUDWIG'S CASTLE

2

Blomberg

Tegernsee

Rottach-Egern

Benediktbeuern

Bad Wiessee

Spitzingsee

Murnau

11

Lenggries

Wallberg

23

Kochelsee

Kochel

Oberammergau

Walchensee

A U S T R I A

Linderhof

Ettal

11

Zugspitze

Garmisch-Partenkirchen

Jenbach

Mittenwald

Schwaz

best fish specialties on the international menu. *See promenade 1, tel. 08151/998–930. Reservations not accepted. AE, MC, V. Closed Tues.*

## Starnbergersee A to Z

### ARRIVING AND DEPARTING

**BY BUS.** The east bank of the lake can be reached by bus from the town of Wolfratshausen, the end of the S-bahn 7 suburban line.

**BY CAR.** Starnberg and the north end of the lake are a 40-minute drive from Munich on the A–95 Autobahn. Follow the signs to Garmisch and take the Starnberg exit. Country roads then skirt the west and east banks of the lake.

**BY TRAIN.** The S-bahn 6 suburban line runs from Munich's central Marienplatz to Starnberg and three other towns on the lake's west bank: Possenhofen, Feldafing, and Tutzing. The journey from Marienplatz to Starnberg takes 35 minutes.

### VISITOR INFORMATION

**Fremdenverkehrsverband** (Wittelsbacher Str. 9 [Am Kirchpl.], D–82319 Starnberg, tel. 08151/13008).

## AMMERSEE

*40 km (25 mi) southwest of Munich.*

The Ammersee is the country cousin of the better-known, more cosmopolitan Starnbergersee, and, accordingly, many Bavarians (and tourists, too) like it all the more. Munich cosmopolites of centuries past thought it too distant for an excursion, not to mention too rustic. So the shores remained relatively free of the villas and parks that ring the Starnbergersee, and even though upscale holiday homes of Munich's moneyed class claim some stretches of the eastern shore, the Ammersee still offers more open areas for bathing and boating than the bigger lake to the west. Bicyclists can circle the 19-km-long (12-mi-long) lake (it's nearly 6 km [4 mi] across at its widest point) on a path that rarely loses sight of the water. Hikers can spread out the tour for two or three days, staying overnight in any of the comfortable inns along the way. Dinghy sailors and windsurfers can zip across in minutes with the help of the Alpine winds that swoop down from the mountains. A ferry cruises the lake at regular intervals during summer, dropping and picking up passengers at several pier stops. Board it at Herrsching.

**Herrsching** has a delightful promenade, part of which winds through the resort's park. The 100-year-old villa that sits so comfortably in the park, overlooking the lake and the Alps beyond, seems as if it were built by Ludwig II, such is the romantic and fanciful mixture of medieval turrets and Renaissance-style facades. It was actually built for the artist Ludwig Scheuermann in the late 19th century and became a favorite meeting place for Munich and Bavarian artists. It is now a municipal cultural center and the scene of chamber-music concerts on some summer weekends.

The Benedictine monastery of **Andechs,** one of southern Bavaria's most famous pilgrimage sites, lies 5 km (3 mi) south of Herrsching. You can reach it on Bus 951 (which also connects Ammersee and Starnbergersee). The 15th-century church is adorned with mid-18th-century rococo decoration and contains religious relics said to have been brought from the Holy Land 1,000 years ago. The church is being renovated completely in the next three years in preparation for the 550th anniversary of the monastery in 2005. Crowds of pilgrims are drawn not only by the beauty of the hilltop monastery but by the beer brewed here (600,000 liters annually). The monastery makes its own cheese as well, and it's an excellent accompaniment to the rich, almost black beer. You can enjoy both at large wooden tables in the monastery tavern or on the terrace outside. The son of the last Austro-Hungarian emperor, Archduke Otto von Habsburg, lives beside the lake. He celebrated his 80th birthday in the church in 1992, with a family party following in the tavern. *Daily 7–7.*

The little town of **Diessen,** with its magnificent baroque abbey church, is at the southwest corner of the lake. Step inside the church to admire its opulent stucco decoration and sumptuous gilt-and-marble altar. Visit in late afternoon, when the light falls sharply on its crisp gray, white, and gold facade, etching the pencil-like tower and spire against the darkening sky over the lake. Don't leave without at least peeping into neighboring St. Stephen's courtyard, its cloisters smothered in wild roses.

## Eating Out

**$$$ LANDHOTEL PIUSHOF.** The family-run Piushof has elegantly Bavarian guest rooms, with lots of oak and hand-carved cupboards. The beamed and pillared restaurant ($$) has an excellent menu of Bavarian specialties. *Schönbichlstr. 18, D–82211 Herrsching, tel. 08152/968–270, fax 08152/968–270. 21 rooms, 2 suites. Restaurant, indoor pool, sauna, massage, tennis court. MC, V.*

**$$–$$$ AMMERSEE HOTEL.** This very comfortable, modern resort hotel has views from an unrivaled position on the lakeside promenade. Rooms overlooking the lake are in big demand and more expensive. The Artis restaurant ($$) has an international menu. *Summerstr. 32, D–82211 Herrsching, tel. 08152/96870, fax 08152/5374. 40 rooms. Restaurant, Weinstube, hot tub, sauna, exercise room. AE, DC, MC, V.*

**$$ HOTEL GARNI ZUR POST.** Families feel particularly at home here, and children amuse themselves at the playground and small deer park. Rooms are Bavarian baroque in style, with heavy drapes and carved farmhouse furniture. *Starnberger Str. 2, D–82346 Andechs, tel. 08152/3433, fax 08152/2303. 32 rooms, 22 with bath. Playground. MC.*

**$$ HOTEL PROMENADE.** From the hotel terrace restaurant you can watch the pleasure boats tie up at the adjacent pier. If you're staying, ask for a room overlooking the lake; they all have geranium-hung balconies. Those under the dormer-broken roof are particularly cozy. *Summerstr. 6, D–82211 Herrsching, tel. 08152/1088, fax 08152/5981. 11 rooms. Restaurant, café. DC, MC, V.*

**Bureau de change**

**Cambio**

**外国為替**

# In this city, you can find money on almost any street.

---

NO-FEE FOREIGN EXCHANGE

---

The Chase Manhattan Bank has over 80 convenient
locations near New York City destinations such as:

        Times Square
        Rockefeller Center
        Empire State Building
        2 World Trade Center
        United Nations Plaza

**Exchange any of 75 foreign currencies**

THE RIGHT RELATIONSHIP IS EVERYTHING.®

## Ammersee A to Z

### ARRIVING AND DEPARTING

**BY BUS.** From the Herrsching train station Bus 952 runs north along the lake, and Bus 951 runs south and continues on to Starnberg in a 40-minute journey.

**BY CAR.** Take Autobahn 96—follow the signs to Lindau—and 20 km (12 mi) west of Munich take the exit for Herrsching, the lake's principal town.

**BY TRAIN.** Herrsching, on the east bank of the lake, is the end of the S-bahn 5 suburban line, a half-hour ride from Munich's Marienplatz.

### VISITOR INFORMATION

**Verkehrsamt** (Bahnhofspl. 2, Herrsching, tel. 08152/5227).

## DACHAU

*20 km (12 mi) northwest of Munich.*

Dachau predates Munich, with records going back to the time of Charlemagne. It's a handsome town, too, built on a hilltop with fine views of Munich and the Alps. A guided tour of the town, including the castle and church, leaves from the Rathaus on Saturday, from May through mid-October. Dachau is better known worldwide as the site of the first Nazi concentration camp, which was built just outside it. Dachau preserves the memory of the camp and the horrors perpetrated there with deep contrition while trying, with commendable discretion, to signal that it also has other points of interest.

The site of the infamous camp, now the **KZ-Gedenkstätte Dachau** (Dachau Concentration Camp Memorial), is just outside town. Photographs, contemporary documents, the few remaining cell blocks, and the grim crematorium (never used) create a somber and moving picture of the camp, where more than 30,000 of the 200,000-plus prisoners lost their lives. A documentary film in English is shown daily at 11:30 and 3:30. To reach the memorial by car, leave the center of the town along Schleissheimerstrasse and turn left into Alte Römerstrasse; the site is on the left. By public transport take Bus 724 or 726 from the Dachau S-bahn train station or the town center. Both stop within a two-minute walk from the site (ask the driver to let you out there). If you are driving from Munich, turn right on the first country road (marked B) before entering Dachau and follow the signs. *Alte Römerstr. 75, tel. 08131/1741. Free. Tues.–Sun. 9–5. Guided English tour June–Aug., Tues.–Sun. 12:30; Sept.–May., weekends 12:30.*

**Schloss Dachau,** the hilltop castle, dominates the town. What you'll see is the one remaining wing of a palace built by the Munich architect Josef Effner for the Wittelsbach ruler Max Emanuel in 1715. During the Napoleonic Wars the palace served as a field hospital, treating French and Russian casualties from the Battle of Austerlitz (1805). The wars made a casualty, too, of the palace, and three of the four wings were demolished by order of King Max Joseph I. What's left is a handsome cream-and-white building, with an elegant pillared and lantern-hung café on the ground floor and a former ballroom above. Concerts are held here, beneath a richly decorated and carved ceiling, with painted panels representing figures from ancient mythology. The east-facing terrace affords panoramic views of Munich and, on fine days, the distant Alps. There's also a 250-year-old *Schlossbrauerei* (castle brewery), which hosts the town's beer and music festival each year in the first two weeks of August. *Schlosspl., tel. 08131/87923. DM 2; tour DM 5. May–Sept., weekends 2–5; tour of town and Schloss May–mid-Oct., Sat. 10:30.*

**St. Jacob,** Dachau's parish church, was built in the early 16th century in late-Renaissance style on the foundations of a 14th-century Gothic structure. Baroque features and a characteristic onion dome were added in the late 17th century. On the south wall you can admire a very fine 17th-century sundial. A visit to the church is included in the guided tour of the town (May–mid-October, Saturday 10:30). *Konrad-Adenauer-Str. 7, Daily 7–7.*

An artists' colony formed here during the 19th century, and the tradition lives on. Picturesque houses line Hermann-Stockmann-Strasse and part of Münchner Strasse, and many of them are still the homes of successful artists. The **Gemäldegalerie** displays the works of many of the town's 19th-century artists. *Konrad-Adenauer-Str. 3, tel. 08131/567–516. DM 3. Wed.–Fri. 11–5, weekends 1–5.*

## Eating Out and Where to Stay

**$–$$** **BRÄUSTÜBERL.** Near the castle, the Bräustüberl has a shady beer garden for lunches and a cozy tavern for year-round Bavarian-style eating and drinking. *Schlossstr. 8, tel. 08131/725. MC. Closed Mon.*

**$–$$** **HÖRHAMMERBRÄU.** You can combine Bavarian farmhouse dishes such as pork knuckle and potato dumplings with the best of home-brewed Dachau beer at this inn. It's not haute cuisine, but the portions will set you up for a whole day's outing to Dachau. *Konrad-Adenauer-Str. 12, tel. 08131/735–711. AE, MC, V.*

**$–$$** **ZIEGLERBRÄU.** Dachau's leading beer tavern, once a 17th-century brewer's home, is a warren of cozy, wood-paneled rooms where you'll probably share a table with a party of locals on a boys' night out. The food is solidly Bavarian, basically varieties of pork, potato, and sausages in all forms. *Konrad-Adenauer-Str. 8, tel. 08131/4074. No credit cards.*

## Dachau A to Z

### ARRIVING AND DEPARTING
**BY CAR.** Take the B–12 country road or the Stuttgart Autobahn to the Dachau exit from Munich.

**BY TRAIN.** Dachau is on the S-bahn 2 suburban line, a 20-minute ride from Munich's Marienplatz.

### VISITOR INFORMATION
**Verkehrsverein Dachau** (Konrad-Adenauer-Str. 1, tel. 08131/84566, www.dachau-info.de).

# LANDSHUT

*64 km (40 mi) north of Munich.*

If fortune had placed Landshut south of Munich, in the protective folds of the Alpine foothills, instead of the same distance north, in the dull flatlands of Lower Bavaria, the historic town would be teeming with tourists. Landshut's geographical misfortune is the discerning visitor's good luck, for the town is never overcrowded, with the possible exception of the three summer weeks every four years when the *Landshuter Hochzeit* (Landshut Wedding) is celebrated. The next celebration is in 2001 (June 30–July 22), and then a visit to Landshut is a must. The festival commemorates the marriage in 1475 of Prince George of Bavaria-Landshut, son of the expressively named Ludwig the Rich, to Princess Hedwig, daughter of the king of Poland. Within its ancient walls, the entire town is swept away in a colorful reconstruction of the event. The wedding procession, with the "bride" and "groom" on horseback, accompanied by pipes and drums and the hurly-burly of a medieval pageant, is held on three consecutive weekends, while a medieval-style fair fills the central streets throughout the three weeks.

Landshut has two magnificent cobblestone market streets. The one in **Altstadt** (Old Town) is one of the most beautiful city streets in Germany; the other is in **Neustadt** (New Town). The two streets run parallel to each other, tracing a course between the Isar River and the heights overlooking the town. A steep path from Altstadt takes you up to **Burg Trausnitz.** This castle was begun in 1204 and accommodated the Wittelsbach dukes of Bavaria-Landshut until 1503. *Tel. 0871/22638. DM 5, including guided tour. Apr.–Sept., daily 9–noon and 1–5; Oct.–Mar., daily 10–noon and 1–4.*

The **Stadtresidenz** in Altstadt was the first Italian Renaissance building of its kind north of the Alps. The Wittelsbachs lived here during the 16th century. The Renaissance facade of the palace forms an almost modest part of the architectural splendor and integrity of the Altstadt, where even the ubiquitous McDonald's has to serve its hamburgers behind a baroque exterior. *Tel. 0871/22638. DM 4. Apr.–Sept., daily 9–noon and 1–5; Oct.–Mar., daily 10–noon and 1–4.*

The **Martinskirche** (St. Martin's), with the tallest brick church tower (436 ft) in the world, soars above the other buildings with its bristling spire. The church contains some magnificent Gothic treasures and a 16th-century carved Madonna. Moreover, it is surely the only church in the world to contain an image of Hitler, albeit in a devilish pose. The Führer and other Nazi leaders are portrayed as executioners in a 1946 stained-glass window showing the martyrdom of St. Kastulus. In the nave of the church is a clear and helpful description of its history and treasures in English. *Tel. 0871/24277. Apr.–Sept., daily 7–6:30; Oct.–Mar., daily 7–5.*

Built into a steep slope of the hill crowned by Burg Trausnitz is an unusual art museum, the **Skulpturenmuseum im Hofberg,** containing the entire collection of the Landshut sculptor Fritz Koenig. His own work forms the permanent central section of the labyrinthine gallery. *Im Hofberg, tel. 0871/89021. DM 6. Tues.–Sun. 10:30–1 and 2–5.*

Freising (at the end of the S-bahn 1 line, a half-hour ride from central Munich) is an ancient episcopal seat and well worth including in a visit to Landshut, 35 km (22 mi) to the northeast.

## Eating Out and Where to Stay

There are several attractive Bavarian-style restaurants in the Altstadt and Neustadt, most of them with beer gardens. Although Landshut brews a fine beer, look for a *Gaststatte* offering a Weihenstephaner, from the world's oldest brewery, in nearby Freising. *Helles* (light) is the most popular beer variety.

**$$$ LINDNER HOTEL KAISERHOF.** The green Isar River rolls outside the bedroom windows of Landshut's most distinctive hotel. Its steep red roof and white facade blend harmoniously with the waterside panorama. The "Herzog Ludwig" restaurant ($$–$$$) serves a sumptuous but reasonably priced lunch buffet and is an elegant place for dinner. *Papiererstr. 2, D–84034, tel. 0871/6870, fax 0871/687–403. 147 rooms. Restaurant, bar, sauna, steam room, exercise room, bicycles, motorbikes. AE, DC, MC, V.*

**$$$  ROMANTIK HOTEL FÜRSTENHOF.** This handsome Landshut city mansion had no difficulty qualifying for inclusion in the Romantik group of hotels—it just breathes romance, from its plush little restaurant ($$–$$$) to the cozy bedrooms. A vine-covered terrace adds charm. *Stethaimerstr. 3, D–84034, tel. 0871/92550, fax 0871/925–544. 24 rooms. Restaurant, sauna. AE, DC, MC, V. www.romantikhotels.com/landshut*

**$$  HOTEL GOLDENE SONNE.** The steeply gabled Renaissance facade of the Golden Sun fronts a hotel of great charm and sleek comfort. It stands in the center of town, near all the sights. Its dining options are a paneled, beamed restaurant, a vaulted cellar, and a courtyard beer garden, where the service is smilingly, helpfully Bavarian. *Neustadt 520, D–84028, tel. 0871/92530, fax 0871/925–3350. 55 rooms. Restaurant, beer garden, pub. AE, DC, MC, V. www.goldenesonne.de*

**$$  SCHLOSS SCHÖNBRUNN.** This historic country mansion is now a luxurious hotel, with many of the original features intact. Rooms in the most historic part of the building are particularly attractive, with huge double beds, and represent excellent value. The handsome house stands in the Schönbrunn district of Landshut, about 2 km (1 mi) from the center. The journey is worthwhile even for the excellent restaurant ($$–$$$), where the menu includes fish from the hotel's own pond. *Schönbrunn 1, D–84036, tel. 0871/95220, fax 0871/952–2222. 33 rooms. Restaurant, bar, beer garden, café. AE, DC, MC, V. www.hotel-schoenbrunn.de*

## Landshut A to Z

### ARRIVING AND DEPARTING

**BY CAR.** Landshut is a 45-minute drive northwest from Munich on either the A–92 Autobahn—follow the signs to Deggendorf—or the B–11 highway.

**BY TRAIN.** Landshut is on the Plattling–Regensburg–Passau line, a 40-minute ride by express train from Munich.

### VISITOR INFORMATION

**Verkehrsverein** (Altstadt 315, tel. 0871/922–050).

# WASSERBURG AM INN

*51 km (30 mi) east of Munich.*

Wasserburg floats like a faded ship of state in a lazy loop of the Inn River, which comes within a few yards of cutting the ancient town off from the wooded slopes of the encroaching countryside. The river caresses the southern limits of the town center, embraces its eastern boundary with rocky banks 200 ft high, returns westward as if looking for a way out of this geographical puzzle, and then heads north in search of its final destination, the Danube. Wasserburg is a perfectly preserved, beautifully set medieval town, once a vitally important trading post but later thankfully ignored by the industrialization that gripped Germany in the 19th century.

You're never more than 100 yards or so from the river in Wasserburg's **Altstadt,** which huddles within the walls of the castle that originally gave the town its name. The almost Italian look is typical of many Inn River towns. Use the north- or east-bank parking lot as the town council is expanding the traffic-free zone. It's only a few minutes' walk to the central Marienplatz. There you'll find Wasserburg's late-Gothic brick **Rathaus.** The Bavarian regional government met here until 1804, deliberating in its beautifully decorated Renaissance *Ratsstube* (council chamber). *Marienpl. DM 1.50. Guided tour Tues.–Fri. at 10, 11, 2, 3, 4; weekends at 10, 11.*

The 14th-century **Frauenkirche** (Church of Our Lady), on Marienplatz, is the town's oldest church. It incorporates an ancient watchtower. The baroque altar frames a Madonna by an unknown 15th-century artist.

Wasserburg's imposing 15th-century parish church, **St. Jakob,** has an intricately carved baroque pulpit dating from 1640.

Next to the 14th-century town gate, at the end of Wasserburg's only bridge, is the unusual **Erstes Imaginäres Museum.** The museum has a collection of more than 500 world-famous paintings, but without an original among them; every single one is a precise copy, executed by various artists. *DM 3. May–Sept., Tues.–Sun. 11–5; Oct.–Apr., Tues.–Sun. 1–5.*

Wasserburg is a convenient base for walks along the banks of the Inn River and into the countryside. A pretty path west leads to the village of **Attel.** Another half hour into the Attel River valley, and you'll reach the enchanting castle-restaurant of **Schloss Hart** (tel. 08039/1774).

## Eating Out and Where to Stay

**$$ HERRENHAUS.** This is one of Wasserburg's oldest houses, with medieval foundations and a centuries-old wine cellar. Many pork dishes with dumplings and sauerkraut are served at the oak tables beneath vaulted ceilings. *Herreng. 17, tel. 08071/2800. MC. Closed Mon. and Aug. No dinner Sun.*

**$$ HOTEL FLETZINGER BRÄU.** Wasserburg's leading hotel began as a brewery, and you can sample local ales in its noisy, friendly tavern. Rooms are large and homey; many have original antiques. *Fletzingerg. 1, D–83512, tel. 08071/90890, fax 08071/909–8177. 40 rooms. Restaurant, beer garden, pub. MC.*

**$ GASTHAUS ZUM LÖWEN.** Simple Bavarian fare is the basis of this sturdy old inn's menu. The roast pork and dumplings are legendary. You can watch the Wasserburg world go by from an outside table. *Marienpl. 10, tel. 08071/7400. No credit cards.*

## Wasserburg A to Z

### ARRIVING AND DEPARTING

**BY CAR.** Take the B–304 from Munich, which leads directly to Wasserburg. It's a 45-minute drive.

**BY TRAIN.** Take either the S-bahn 4 suburban line to Ebersberg and change to a local train to Wasserburg, or the Salzburg express, changing at Grafing Bahnhof to the local line. Both trips take 90 minutes.

### VISITOR INFORMATION

**Verkehrsamt** (Rathauspl. 1, D–83512 Wasserburg am Inn, tel. 08071/1050).

# where to stay

**THOUGH MUNICH HAS A VAST NUMBER** of hotels in all price ranges, many are fully booked year-round; this is a major trade and convention city as well as a prime tourist destination. If you're visiting during Mode Wochen (Fashion Weeks), in March and September, or during Oktoberfest at the end of September, make reservations at least six months in advance.

Some of the large, very expensive ($$$$) hotels that cater to expense-account business travelers have very attractive weekend discount rates—sometimes as much as 50% below normal prices. Conversely, regular rates can go up during big trade fairs.

Munich's two tourist information offices—at the main railway station and in the city center (Marienplatz, in the Rathaus)—make hotel bookings. Telephone lines are usually busy, so your best bet is to visit one of the offices personally.

| CATEGORY | COST* |
|---|---|
| $$$$ | over DM 300 |
| $$$ | DM 200–DM 300 |
| $$ | DM 140–DM 200 |
| $ | under DM 140 |

*All prices are for two people in a double room, including tax and service charge.*

**$$$$ BAYERISCHER HOF.** Germany's most respected family-owned hotel, the Bayerischer Hof began its rich history by hosting Ludwig I's guests. Public rooms are grandly laid out with marble, antiques, and oil paintings. Laura Ashley–decorated rooms face the city's

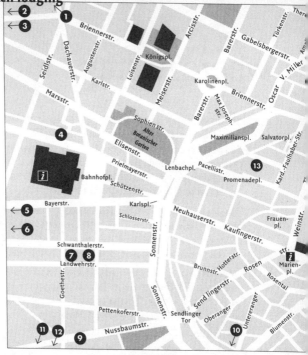

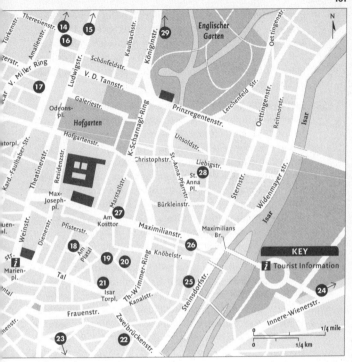

Olympic, **10**

Pannonia Hotel
Königin
Elisabeth, **1**

Park–Hotel
Theresienhöhe, **6**

Platzl, **18**

Rafael, **19**

Splendid, **26**

Torbräu, **21**

Vier Jahreszeiten
Kempinski, **27**

skyline of towers. Rooms facing the interior courtyard are the least expensive and begin at DM 495. Nightlife is built into the hotel, with Trader Vic's bar and dancing at the Night Club. *Promenadepl. 2–6, D–80333, tel. 089/21200, fax 089/212–0906. 306 rooms, 45 suites. 3 restaurants, bar, pool, beauty salon, massage, sauna, nightclub, parking (fee). AE, DC, MC, V. www.bayerischerhof.de*

**$$$$** **PARK-HOTEL THERESIENHÖHE.** Even the mansard rooms are spacious and airy in this newly constructed hotel on the edge of Munich's fairgrounds and Oktoberfest site. In fact, the hotel claims that none of its rooms is less than 400 square ft. Suites are larger than many luxury apartments, and some of them come with small kitchens. The sleek, modern rooms are mostly decorated with light woods and pastel-color fabrics and carpeting; larger rooms and suites get a lot of light, thanks to the floor-to-ceiling windows. Families are particularly welcome, and a baby-sitting service is provided. *Parkstr. 31, D–80339, tel. 089/519–950, fax 089/ 5199–5420. 35 rooms. Restaurant, bar, baby-sitting. AE, DC, MC, V.*

**$$$$** **PLATZL.** The Platzl has won awards and wide recognition for its ecologically aware management. It stands in the historic heart of Munich, near the famous Hofbräuhaus beer hall and a couple of minutes' walk from Marienplatz and many other landmarks. Its *Pfistermühle* restaurant, with 16th-century vaulting, is one of the area's oldest and most historic. *Sparkassenstr. 10, D–80331, tel. 089/237–030, 800/448–8355 in the U.S., fax 089/2370–3800. 167 rooms. Restaurant, bar, sauna, steam room, exercise room, parking (fee). AE, DC, MC, V. www.platzl.de*

**$$$$** ★ **RAFAEL.** Germany's leading hotel reviewers have named the Rafael the country's top grand hotel, and its restaurant, Mark's, also ranks among the country's best. The hotel occupies a beautifully renovated neo-Renaissance building that was a high-society ballroom in the late 19th century. Today it recaptures some of that bygone era with 24-hour service, including such personalized amenities as in-house butlers. Rooms are individually furnished and extravagantly decorated, in addition to offering many extras, including fax machines. *Neuturmstr. 1, D–80331, tel. 089/290–980, fax 089/222–539. 67 rooms, 6 suites. Restaurant, 2 bars, pool, sauna. AE, DC, MC, V. www.rafaelhotel.de*

$$$$ **VIER JAHRESZEITEN KEMPINSKI.** The Four Seasons has been
★ playing host to the world's wealthy and titled for more than a century. It has an unbeatable location on Maximilianstrasse, Munich's premier shopping street, only a few minutes' walk from the heart of the city. Elegance and luxury set the tone throughout; many rooms have handsome antique pieces. The Bistro Eck is on the main floor, and the Theater bar/restaurant is in the cellar. *Maximilianstr. 17, D–80539, tel. 089/21250, 516/794–2670 for Kempinski Reservation Service, fax 089/2125–2000. 268 rooms, 48 suites. 2 restaurants, piano bar, pool, massage, sauna, exercise room, car rental, parking (fee). AE, DC, MC, V. www.Kempinski-Vierjahreszeiten.de*

$$$–$$$$ **BAUER.** Extensive renovations in 1998 and 1999 have elevated the family-run Bauer from country-inn status to a very comfortable hotel indeed, although none of its Bavarian charm has been lost. Located 10 km (6 mi) from the city center, the hotel is best for those traveling by car, although an S-bahn station with rapid access to the center of Munich is only a short walk. *Münchnerstr. 6, D–85622 Feldkirchen, tel. 089/90980, fax 089/909–8414. 100 rooms. Restaurant, café, indoor pool, sauna. AE, DC, MC, V.*

$$$–$$$$ **EDEN HOTEL WOLFF.** Chandeliers and dark-wood paneling in the public rooms make for the old-fashioned elegance of this downtown favorite. It's directly across the street from the train station and near the Theresienwiese fairgrounds. The rooms come with plush comforts, and most are spacious. You can dine on excellent Bavarian specialties in the intimate Zirbelstube restaurant. *Arnulfstr. 4, D–80335, tel. 089/551–150, fax 089/5511–*

5555. 209 rooms, 7 suites. Restaurant, bar, café, exercise room, parking (fee). AE, DC, MC, V. www.ehw.de

**$$$–$$$$ TORBRÄU.** In this snug hotel you'll sleep under the shadow of one of Munich's ancient city gates—the 14th-century Isartor. The location is excellent as it's midway between the Marienplatz and the Deutsches Museum (and around the corner from the Hofbräuhaus). The hotel has been run by the same family for more than a century. Comfortable rooms are decorated in a plush and ornate Italian style. Its Italian restaurant, La Famiglia, is one of the best in the area. Tal 41, D–80331, tel. 089/242–340, fax 089/ 234–235. 83 rooms, 3 suites. Restaurant, café, in-room data ports, sauna, exercise room, bowling, meeting rooms. AE, MC, V. www.torbraeu.de

**$$$ ADMIRAL.** The small, privately owned Admiral enjoys a quiet ★ side-street location and its own garden, close to the Isar River and Deutsches Museum. Many of the simply furnished and warmly decorated bedrooms have a balcony overlooking the garden. Bowls of fresh fruit are part of the friendly welcome awaiting guests. The breakfast buffet is a dream, complete with homemade jams, in-season strawberries, and Italian and French delicacies. Kohlstr. 9, D–80469, tel. 089/216–350, fax 089/293–674. 33 rooms. Bar, parking (fee). AE, DC, MC, V. www.hotel-admiral.de

**$$$ ADRIA.** This modern, comfortable hotel is ideally set in the upmarket area of Lehel, in the middle of Munich's museum quarter. Rooms are large and tastefully decorated, with old prints on the pale-pink walls, Oriental rugs on the floors, and flowers beside the double beds. A spectacular breakfast buffet (including a glass of sparkling wine) is included in the room rate. There's no hotel restaurant, but the area is rich in good restaurants, bistros, and bars. Liebigstr. 8a, D–80538, tel. 089/293–081, fax 089/ 227–015. 46 rooms, 45 with bath. AE, MC, V.

**$$$ ADVOKAT.** Owner Kevin Voigt designed much of the furniture of his exquisite new hotel and had it made by Italian craftsmen. The Italian touch is everywhere, from the sleek, minimalist lines of the bedroom furniture and fittings to the choice prints and modern Florentine mirrors on the walls. If you value modern taste over plush luxury, this is the hotel for you. *Baaderstr. 1, D–80469, tel. 089/216–310, fax 089/216–3190. 50 rooms. AE, DC, MC, V. www.hotel-advokat.de*

**$$$ ARABELLASHERATON AIRPORT.** This is not your typical airport hotel—it's a three-story, red-roof country-house-style building surrounded by greenery. The first-class lodging is only five minutes from the Franz Josef Strauss Airport, and the hotel operates a courtesy shuttle bus. Mostly businesspeople stay here, and there are plenty of leisure facilities. Rooms are furnished in light pinewood, with Laura Ashley fabrics. *Freisingerstr. 80, D–85445 Schwaig, tel. 089/9272–2750, fax 089/9272–2800. 162 rooms, 8 suites. 2 restaurants, bar, indoor pool, sauna, steam room, exercise room, meeting rooms, airport shuttle. AE, DC, MC, V. www.arabellasheraton.de*

**$$$ ERZGIESSEREI EUROPE.** Its location on a dull little street in an uninteresting section of the city is this hotel's only drawback, but even that is easily overcome—the nearby subway whisks you in five minutes to central Karlsplatz, convenient to the pedestrian shopping area and the main railway station. Rooms in this attractive, modern hotel are particularly bright, decorated in soft pastels with good reproductions on the walls. The cobblestone garden café is a haven of peace. *Erzgiessereistr. 15, D–80335, tel. 089/126–820, fax 089/123–6198. 105 rooms, 1 suite. Restaurant, bar, café, parking (fee). AE, DC, MC, V. www.top-hotels.de/erzeurope*

**$$$ HOTEL CONCORDE.** The centrally located Concorde wants to do its bit toward relieving traffic congestion, so guests who arrive from the airport on the S-bahn can exchange their ticket at the reception desk for a welcome champagne or cocktail. The nearest S-bahn station (Isartor) is only a two-minute walk. Rooms were redecorated in 1999, in pastel tones and light woods. Fresh flowers and bright prints add a colorful touch. A large breakfast buffet is served in its stylish, mirrored Salon Margarita. *Herrnstr. 38, D–80539, tel. 089/*

224–515, fax 089/228–3282. *67 rooms, 4 suites. Lounge. AE, DC, MC, V.*

**$$$ OLYMPIC.** The English-style entrance lobby, with its leather easy chairs and mahogany fittings, is an attractive introduction to this friendly small hotel, a beautifully converted turn-of-the-century mansion, amid the bars and boutiques of the colorful district between Sendlinger Tor and Isartor. Most of the rooms, tucked away beneath the steep eaves of the handsome house, look out over a quiet interior courtyard. *Hans-Sachs-Str. 4, D–80469, tel. 089/231–890, fax 089/231–89199. 38 rooms, 3 apartments. Parking (fee). AE, DC, MC, V.*

**$$$ PANNONIA HOTEL KÖNIGIN ELISABETH.** A bright, modern interior, with emphasis on the color pink, lies behind the protected neoclassical facade of this Pannonia-group hotel, a 15-minute tram ride northwest of the city center. Children under 12 stay free in their parents' room. *Leonrodstr. 79, D–80636, tel. 089/126–860, fax 089/1268–6459. 79 rooms. Restaurant, bar, beer garden, hot tub, sauna, steam room, exercise room. AE, DC, MC, V. Closed late Dec.–early Jan.* www.pannonia-hotels.com

**$$$ SPLENDID.** Chandelier-hung public rooms, complete with Louis XVI–era antiques and Oriental rugs, give this small hotel something of the atmosphere of a 19th-century city residence. Bedrooms are all individually furnished. Breakfast is served in the small courtyard in summer and snacks are available at the bar. The chic shops of the Maximilianstrasse are a five-minute stroll. *Maximilianstr. 54, D–80538, tel. 089/296–606, fax 089/291–3176. 32 rooms, 7 suites. Bar. AE, DC, MC, V.*

**$$–$$$ BRACK.** Oktoberfest revelers value the Brack's proximity to the beer festival grounds, and its location—on a busy, tree-lined thoroughfare just south of the center—is handy for city attractions. Rooms are furnished in light, friendly veneers and are soundproof (a useful feature during Oktoberfest) and have amenities such as hair dryers and cable TV. The buffet breakfast will set you up for the day. *Lindwurmstr. 153, D–80337, tel. 089/747–2550, fax 089/7472–5599. 50 rooms. Free parking. AE, DC, MC, V. www.hotel-brack.de*

**$$–$$$**  **GÄSTEHAUS AM ENGLISCHEN GARTEN.** Reserve well in advance
★  for a room at this popular converted water mill, more than 200 years old, adjoining the Englischer Garten. The hotel, complete with ivy-clad walls and shutter-framed windows, is only a five-minute walk from the bars, shops, and restaurants of Schwabing. Be sure to ask for one of the 12 nostalgically old-fashioned rooms in the main building; a modern annex down the road has 13 apartments, all with cooking facilities. In summer breakfast is served on the terrace of the main house, which has a garden on an island in the old millrace. *Liebergesellstr. 8, D–80802, tel. 089/383–9410, fax 089/3839–4133. 12 rooms, 6 with bath or shower; 13 apartments. Free parking. AE, DC, MC, V.*

**$$–$$$**  **HOTEL MIRABELL.** This family-run hotel reports that it has "many
★  tourists from the USA," who like its friendly atmosphere, central location (between the main railway station and the Oktoberfest fairgrounds), and reasonable room rates. Three apartments are for small groups or families. All rooms have TVs and phones, and are furnished in modern, light woods and bright prints. The restaurant serves breakfast only, but snacks can be ordered at the bar. *Landwehrstr. 42 (entrance on Goethestr.), D–80336, tel. 089/549–1740, fax 089/550–3701. 65 rooms, 3 apartments. Bar, café. AE, MC, V.*

**$$–$$$**  **MAYER.** If you are willing to sacrifice location for good value, head for this family-run hotel 25 minutes by suburban train from the Hauptbahnhof. The Mayer's first-class comforts and facilities cost about half of what you'd pay at similar lodgings in town. Built in the 1970s, it is furnished in Bavarian country-rustic style—lots of pine and green and red, and check fabrics. The Mayer is a 10-minute walk or a short taxi ride from Germering station on the S-5 line, eight stops west of the Hauptbahnhof. *Augsburgerstr. 45, Germering D–82110, tel. 089/844–071, fax 089/844–094. 65 rooms. Restaurant, indoor pool. AE, DC, MC, V. www.hotel-mayer.de*

**$$ CARLTON.** This is a favorite of many diplomats: a small, elegant, discreet hotel on a quiet side street in the best area of downtown Munich. The American and British consulates are a short walk away, and so are some of the liveliest Schwabing bars and restaurants. Art galleries, museums, and movie theaters are also in the immediate area. Rooms are on the small side but comfortable. A glass of champagne is included in the complimentary buffet breakfast. *Fürstenstr. 12, D–80333, tel. 089/282–061, fax 089/284–391. 50 rooms. Sauna. AE, DC, MC, V.*

**$$ JAGDSCHLOSS.** Once a hunting lodge, the 100-year-old Jagdschloss, in Munich's leafy Obermenzing suburb, is today a delightful hotel. The rustic look has been retained, with lots of original woodwork and white stucco. Many of the comfortable pastel-tone bedrooms have wooden balconies with flower boxes bursting with color. Doubly sprung mattresses assure a good night's sleep. In the beamed restaurant or sheltered beer garden you'll be served Bavarian specialties by a staff dressed in traditional lederhosen (shorts in summer, breeches in winter). *Alte Allee 21, D–81245 München-Obermenzing, tel. 089/820–820, fax 089/8208–2100. 22 rooms, 1 suite. Restaurant, beer garden, playground, free parking. MC, V. www.weber-gastronomie.de*

**$$ KRIEMHILD.** If you're traveling with children, you'll appreciate this welcoming, family-run pension in the western suburb of Nymphenburg, near parks and gardens. It's a 10-minute walk from Schloss Nymphenburg and around the corner from the Hirschgarten Park, site of one of the city's best beer gardens. The tram ride (No. 16 or 17) from downtown is 10 minutes. The buffet breakfast is included in the rate. *Guntherstr. 16, D–80639, tel. 089/171–1170, fax 089/1711–1755. 18 rooms. Bar, free parking. AE, MC, V. www.kriemhild.de*

**$$ KURPFALZ.** Guests have praised the friendly welcome and service they receive at this centrally placed and affordable lodging. Rooms are comfortable, if furnished in a manner only slightly better than functional, and all are equipped with satellite TV. The main train station and Oktoberfest grounds are both a 10-minute walk, and the area is rich in restaurants, bars, and movie theaters. *Schwantalerstr. 121, D–80339, tel. 089/540–986, fax 089/5409–8811. 44 rooms with shower. Bar, in-room data ports. AE, MC, V.*

**$ FÜRST.** On a quiet street just off Odeonsplatz, on the edge of the
★ university quarter, this basic, clean guest house is constantly busy with families and students traveling on a budget. A cheerful touch is the collection of pictures in the pension's own art gallery. *Kardinal-Döpfner-Str. 8, D–80333, tel. 089/281–044, fax 089/280–860. 19 rooms, 12 with bath. No credit cards.*

**$ HOTEL PENSION AM SIEGESTOR.** This modest but very appealing
★ pension takes up three floors of a fin-de-siècle mansion between the Siegestor monument, on Leopoldstrasse, and the university. An ancient wood-paneled, glass-door elevator brings you to the fourth-floor reception desk. Most of the simply furnished rooms face the impressive Arts Academy across the street. Rooms on the fifth floor are particularly cozy, tucked up under the eaves. *Akademiestr. 5, D–80799, tel. 089/399–550 or 089/399–551, fax 089/ 343–050. 20 rooms. No credit cards.*

**$ HOTEL-PENSION BECK.** American and British guests receive a
★ particularly warm welcome from the Anglophile owner of the rambling, friendly Beck (she and her pet canary are a regular presence). Bright new carpeting, with matching pinewood furniture, gives rooms a cheerful touch. The pension has a prime location in the heart of fashionable Lehel (convenient to museums and the Englischer Garten). *Thierschstr. 36, D–80538, tel. 089/220– 708 or 089/225–768, fax 089/220–925. 44 rooms, 7 with shower. MC, V. www.bst-online.de/pension.beck*

**$ HOTEL-PENSION MARIANDL.** The American armed forces commandeered this turn-of-the-20th-century neo-Gothic mansion in May 1945 and established Munich's first postwar nightclub, the Femina, on the ground floor (now a charming café-restaurant, ☞

# Hotel How-Tos

Where you stay does make a difference. Do you prefer a modern high-rise or an intimate B&B? A center-city location or the quiet suburbs? What facilities do you want? Sort through your priorities, then price it all out.

**HOW TO GET A DEAL** After you've chosen a likely candidate or two, phone them directly and price a room for your travel dates. Then call the hotel's toll-free number and ask the same questions. Also try consolidators and hotel-room discounters. You won't hear the same rates twice. On the spot, make a reservation as soon as you are quoted a price you want to pay.

**PROMISES, PROMISES** If you have special requests, make them when you reserve. Get written confirmation of any promises.

**SETTLE IN** Upon arriving, make sure everything works—lights and lamps, TV and radio, sink, tub, shower, and anything else that matters. Report any problems immediately. And don't wait until you need extra pillows or blankets or an ironing board to call housekeeping. Also check out the fire emergency instructions. Know where to find the fire exits, and make sure your companions do, too.

**IF YOU NEED TO COMPLAIN** Be polite but firm. Explain the problem to the person in charge. Suggest a course of action. If you aren't satisfied, repeat your requests to the manager. Document everything: Take pictures and keep a written record of who you've spoken with, when, and what was said. Contact your travel agent, if he made the reservations.

**KNOW THE SCORE** When you go out, take your hotel's business cards (one for everyone in your party). If you have extras, you can give them out to new acquaintances who want to call you.

**TIP UP FRONT** For special services, a tip or partial tip in advance can work wonders.

**USE ALL THE HOTEL RESOURCES** A concierge can make difficult things easy. But a desk clerk, bellhop, or other hotel employee who's friendly, smart, and ambitious can often steer you straight as well. A gratuity is in order if the advice is helpful.

Cafe am Beethovenplatz in Eating Out). Most rooms are mansion size, with high ceilings and large windows overlooking a leafy avenue. The Oktoberfest grounds and the main railway station are both a 10-minute walk. *Goethestr. 51, D–80336, tel. 089/534–108, fax 089/5440–4396. 28 rooms. Café-restaurant. No credit cards.*

# PRACTICAL INFORMATION

## Addresses

In this book the words for street (*Strasse*) and alley (*Gasse*) are abbreviated as str. and g. within italicized service information. Brüdergasse will appear as Brüderg., for example.

## Air Travel

### BOOKING

When you book, **look for nonstop flights** and **remember that "direct" flights stop at least once.** Try to avoid connecting flights, which require a change of plane.

### CARRIERS

Delta, LTU International Airways, Lufthansa, United, and US Airways fly direct to Munich. The rest of the airlines listed fly to nearby cities, where you can make a connection.

➤ MAJOR AIRLINES: **American** (tel. 800/433–7300). **Continental** (tel. 800/525–0280). **Delta** (tel. 800/241–4141). **LTU International Airways** (tel. 800/888–0200). **Lufthansa** (tel. 800/645–3880). **Northwest** (tel. 800/225–2525). **TWA** (tel. 800/221–2000). **United** (tel. 800/241–6522). **US Airways** (tel. 800/428–4322).

➤ FROM THE U.K.: **British Airways** (tel. 0345/222–111). **Lufthansa** (10 Old Bond St., London W1X 4EN, tel. 020/8750–3300 or 0345/737–747).

➤ DOMESTIC AIRLINES: **Deutsche BA** (tel. 089/9759–1500). **LTU** (tel. 0211/941–8888). **Lufthansa** (tel. 01803/803–803).

### CHECK-IN & BOARDING

The first to get bumped from an overbooked flight are passengers who checked in late and those flying on discounted tickets, so **get to the gate and check in as early as possible,** especially during peak periods.

Always **bring a government-issued photo ID to the airport.**
You may be asked to show it before you are allowed to check
in.

## CUTTING COSTS

The least expensive airfares to Germany must usually be
purchased in advance and are nonrefundable. It's smart to **call
a number of airlines, and when you are quoted a good price,
book it on the spot**—the same fare may not be available the
next day. Always **check different routings** and look into using
different airports. Travel agents, especially low-fare specialists
(☞ Discounts & Deals, *below*), are helpful.

Consolidators are another good source. They buy tickets for
scheduled international flights at reduced rates from the airlines,
then sell them at prices that beat the best fare available directly
from the airlines, usually without restrictions. Sometimes you
can even get your money back if you need to return the ticket.
Carefully read the fine print detailing penalties for changes and
cancellations, and **confirm your consolidator reservation with
the airline.**

➤ CONSOLIDATORS: **Cheap Tickets** (tel. 800/377–1000). **Discount
Airline Ticket Service** (tel. 800/576–1600). **Unitravel** (tel. 800/325–
2222). **Up & Away Travel** (tel. 212/889–2345). **World Travel
Network** (tel. 800/409–6753).

## ENJOYING THE FLIGHT

For more legroom, **request an emergency-aisle seat.** Don't sit
in the row in front of the emergency aisle or in front of a
bulkhead, where seats may not recline. If you have dietary
concerns, **ask for special meals when booking.** On long
flights try to maintain a normal routine in order to help fight jet
lag. At night, **get some sleep.** By day, **eat light meals, drink
water** (not alcohol), and **move around the cabin** to stretch
your legs.

## HOW TO COMPLAIN

If your baggage goes astray or your flight goes awry, complain right away. Most carriers require that you **file a claim immediately.**

➤ AIRLINE COMPLAINTS: **U.S. Department of Transportation Aviation Consumer Protection Division** (C-75, Room 4107, Washington, DC 20590, tel. 202/366–2220, www.dot.gov/airconsumer). **Federal Aviation Administration Consumer Hotline** (tel. 800/322–7873).

## WITHIN GERMANY

Germany's internal air network is excellent, with frequent flights linking all major cities in about an hour. Services are operated by Deutsche BA, a British Airways subsidiary, Lufthansa, and LTU.

# Airports & Transfers

### AIRPORT

Flughafen München (Munich International Airport) is 28 km (17 mi) northeast of the city center, between the small towns of Freising and Erding.

➤ INFORMATION: **Munich International Airport** (tel. 089/9752–1313).

### BETWEEN THE AIRPORT AND DOWNTOWN

A fast train service links the airport with Munich's main train station. The S-1 and S-8 lines operate from a terminal directly beneath the airport's arrival and departure halls. Trains leave every 10 minutes, and the journey takes around 40 minutes. Several intermediate stops are made, including the Ostbahnhof (convenient for lodgings east of the Isar River) and such city-center stations as Marienplatz. A one-way ticket costs DM 14.40, or DM 12 if you purchase a multiple-use "strip" ticket. A family of up to five (two adults and three children under 15) can make the trip for DM 26 by buying a Tageskarte ticket.

The bus service is slower and more expensive (DM 16) than the S-bahn link and is only recommended if you have a lot of luggage. A taxi from the airport costs between DM 90 and DM 100. During rush hours (7–10 and 4–7), allow up to an hour of traveling time. If you're driving from the airport to the city, take route A–9 and follow the signs for MÜNCHEN STADTMITTE. If you're driving to the airport from the city center, head north through Schwabing, join the A–9 Autobahn at the Frankfurter Ring intersection, and follow the signs for the airport (FLUGHAFEN).

## DUTY-FREE SHOPPING

You can purchase duty-free goods when traveling between any EU country, such as Germany, and a non-EU country. Duty-free (also called tax-free) shops at German airports are operated by the firm of Gebrüder Heinemann, which boasts that its prices (even for Scotch whisky) are "15 to 20% cheaper" than in the London duty-free shops. The big sellers, as at most duty-free shops, are perfumes and cosmetics, liquor, and tobacco products.

# Biking

Munich and its environs are easily navigated on two wheels. The city is threaded with a network of specially designated bike paths, and bikes are allowed on the S-bahn. A free map showing all bike trails is available at all city tourist offices. Bikes can be rented at Radl-Discount, Aktiv-Rad, and the Hauptbahnhof (from April through October). Some S-bahn and mainline stations also rent bikes. A list of stations that offer the service is available from the Deutsche Bahn. The cost is DM 6–DM 8 a day if you've used public transportation to reach the station; otherwise it's DM 10–DM 12, depending on the type of bike.

➤ BIKE RENTALS: **Radl-Discount** (Benediktbeurerstr. 20–22, tel. 089/724–2351; **Trappentreustr. 10,** tel. 089/506–285). **Aktiv-Rad** (Hans-Sachs-Str. 7, tel. 089/266–506). **Hauptbahnhof** (Radius Touristik, opposite platform 31, tel. 089/596–113).

## Bus Travel

Long-distance buses arrive at and depart from the north side of the main train station. A taxi stand is right next to it.

## Business Hours

Catholicism gives Bavaria more religious holidays than the other states of Germany. Otherwise, business hours are consistent throughout the country. Many towns' visitor information offices close by 4 during the week and might not be open on weekends.

### BANKS & OFFICES

Banks are generally open weekdays from 8:30 or 9 to 3 or 4 (5 or 6 on Thursday), sometimes with a lunch break of about an hour at smaller branches. Banks at airports and main train stations open as early as 6:30 AM and close as late as 10:30 PM.

### MUSEUMS & SIGHTS

Most museums are open from Tuesday to Sunday 10–5. Some close for an hour or more at lunch. Many stay open until 8 or 9 on Wednesday or Thursday.

### SHOPS

Department stores and larger stores are generally open from 9 or 9:15 to 8 weekdays and until 4 on Saturday. Smaller shops and some department stores in smaller towns close at 6 or 6:30 on weekdays and as early as 1 on Saturday. Visit a department store in the morning or early afternoon to avoid crowds.

## Car Rental

All Hauptbahnhof (train station) offices are in the mezzanine-level gallery above the Deutsche Bahn information and ticket center. Airport offices are in the central area, Zentralbereich.

Rates with the major car-rental companies begin at about $45 per day and $220 per week for an economy car with a manual transmission and unlimited mileage. This does not include tax on car rentals, which is 16%. Volkswagen, Opel, and Mercedes are some standard brands of rentals; most rentals are manual, so if you want an automatic, be sure to **request one in advance.** If you're traveling with children, don't forget to **arrange for a car seat** when you reserve.

➤ MAJOR AGENCIES: **Alamo** (tel. 800/522–9696; 020/8759–6200 in the U.K.). **Avis** (tel. 800/331–1084; 800/879–2487 in Canada; 02/9353–9000 in Australia; 09/525–1982 in New Zealand; 0610 in Germany). **Budget** (tel. 800/527–0700; 0870/607–5000 in the U.K., through affiliate Europcar). **Dollar** (tel. 800/800–6000; 0124/622–0111 in the U.K., through affiliate Sixt Kenning; 02/9223–1444 in Australia). **Hertz** (tel. 800/654–3001; 800/263–0600 in Canada; 020/8897–2072 in the U.K.; 02/9669–2444 in Australia; 09/256–8690 in New Zealand; 01805/8000 in Germany). **National Car Rental** (tel. 800/227–7368; 020/8680–4800 in the U.K., where it is known as NationalEurope).

➤ WITHIN MUNICH: **Avis** (Airport, tel. 089/975–97600; Hauptbahnhof, tel. 089/550–2251; Nymphenburgerstr. 61, tel. 089/1260–0020; Balanstr. 74, tel. 089/403–091). **Europcar** (Airport, tel. 089/973–5020; Hauptbahnhof, tel. 089/550–1341; Hirtenstr. 14, tel. 089/557–145). **Hertz** (Airport, tel. 089/978–860; Hauptbahnhof, tel. 089/550–2256; Nymphenburgerstr. 81, tel. 089/129–5001). **Sixt** (Airport, tel. 089/526–2525; Hauptbahnhof, tel. 089/550–2447; Seitzstr. 9, tel. 089/223–333).

## CUTTING COSTS

To get the best deal, **book through a travel agent who will shop around.**

Do **look into wholesalers,** companies that do not own fleets but rent in bulk from those that do and often offer better rates than traditional car-rental operations. Payment must be made before you leave home.

➤ WHOLESALERS: **Auto Europe** (tel. 207/842–2000 or 800/223–5555, fax 800–235–6321, www.autoeurope.com). **DER Travel Services** (9501 W. Devon Ave., Rosemont, IL 60018, tel. 800/782–

2424, fax 800/282–7474 for information, 800/860–9944 for brochures, www.dertravel.com). **Kemwel Holiday Autos** (tel. 800/678–0678, fax 914/825–3160, www.kemwel.com).

## INSURANCE

When driving a rented car, you are generally responsible for any damage to or loss of the vehicle. Before you rent, see what coverage your personal auto-insurance policy and credit cards already provide.

Collision policies that car-rental companies sell for European rentals usually do not include stolen-vehicle coverage. Before you buy it, check your existing policies—you may already be covered.

## REQUIREMENTS & RESTRICTIONS

In Germany your own driver's license is acceptable, but an International Driver's Permit is a good idea; it's available from the American or Canadian automobile association and, in the United Kingdom, from the Automobile Association or Royal Automobile Club. These international permits are universally recognized, and having one in your wallet may save you a problem with the local authorities. In Germany you must be 21 to rent a car, and rates may be higher if you're under 25.

## SURCHARGES

Before you pick up a car in one city and leave it in another, **ask about drop-off charges or one-way service fees,** which can be substantial. Note, too, that some rental agencies charge extra if you return the car before the time specified in your contract. To avoid a hefty refueling fee, **fill the tank just before you turn in the car,** but be aware that gas stations near the rental outlet may overcharge.

# Car Travel

Entry formalities for motorists are few: All you need is proof of insurance, an international car-registration document, and a

U.S. or Canadian driver's license (an international license is helpful but not a must). If you or your car are from an EU country, Norway, or Switzerland, all you need is your domestic license and proof of insurance. All foreign cars must have a country sticker.

To reach Munich from the north (Nürnberg or Frankfurt), leave the autobahn at the Schwabing exit. From Stuttgart and the west, the autobahn ends at Obermenzing, Munich's most westerly suburb. The autobahns from Salzburg and the east, Garmisch and the south, and Lindau and the southwest all join the Mittlerer Ring (city beltway). When leaving any autobahn, follow the signs reading STADTMITTE for downtown Munich.

## AUTO CLUBS

Allgemeiner Deutscher Automobil-Club (ADAC), one of Germany's three principal automobile clubs, is in Munich.

➤ **INFORMATION: ADAC** (Am Westpark 8, D–81373 Munich, fax 089/7676–2801).

## EMERGENCY SERVICES

ADAC operates tow trucks on all autobahns; they also have emergency telephones every 2 km (1 mi). On minor roads **go to the nearest call box and dial 01802/222–222** (if you have a mobile phone, just dial 222–222) Ask, in English, for road-service assistance. Help is free (with the exception of materials) if the work is carried out by the ADAC. If the ADAC has to use a subcontractor for the work, charges are made for time, mileage, and materials.

## GASOLINE

Gasoline (petrol) costs are between DM 1.50 and DM 2 per liter. Most German cars run on lead-free fuel. Some models use diesel fuel, so if you are renting a car, **find out which fuel the car takes.** Pumps marked Bleifrei contain unleaded gas.

## RULES OF THE ROAD

In Germany you **drive on the right,** and road signs give distances in kilometers. There is no speed limit on autobahns, although drivers are advised to keep below 130 kph (80 mph). Speed limits on country roads vary from 80 to 100 kph (50 to 60 mph). Alcohol limits on drivers are equivalent to two small beers or a quarter of a liter of wine (blood-alcohol level .05%). Note that **seat belts must be worn at all times by front- and backseat passengers.** Passing is permitted on the left side only. Headlights, not parking lights, are required during inclement weather.

# Children in Germany

Munich's tourist offices have booklets of information for younger visitors, and playgrounds are around virtually every corner. If you are renting a car, don't forget to **arrange for a car seat** when you reserve.

### BABY-SITTING

For recommended local sitters, **check with your hotel desk.** Updated lists of well-screened baby-sitters are also available from most local tourist offices. Rates are usually between DM 20 and DM 30 per hour. Many large department stores in Germany provide baby-sitting facilities or areas where children can play while their parents shop.

### FLYING

If your children are two or older, **ask about children's airfares.** As a general rule, infants under two not occupying a seat fly at greatly reduced fares or even for free. When booking, **confirm carry-on allowances** if you're traveling with infants. In general, for babies charged 10% of the adult fare you are allowed one carry-on bag and a collapsible stroller; if the flight is full, the stroller may have to be checked, or you may be limited to fewer carry-ons.

# Money From Home In Minutes.

If you're stuck for cash on your travels, don't panic. Millions of people trust Western Union to transfer money in minutes to 176 countries and over 78,000 locations worldwide. Our record of safety and reliability is second to none. For more information, call Western Union: USA 1-800-325-6000, Canada 1-800-235-0000. Wherever you are, you're never far from home.

**www.westernunion.com**

**WESTERN UNION | MONEY TRANSFER®**

*The fastest way to send money worldwide.*

# Find America
## WITH A COMPASS

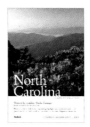
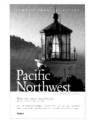

Written by local authors and illustrated throughout with spectacular color images from regional photographers, these companion guides reveal the character and culture of more than 35 of America's most spectacular destinations. Perfect for residents who want to explore their own backyards, and visitors who want an insider's perspective on the history, heritage, and all there is to see and do.

**Fodor's** COMPASS AMERICAN GUIDES

*At bookstores everywhere.*

## LODGING

Most hotels in Germany allow children under a certain age to stay in their parents' room at no extra charge, but others charge for them as extra adults; be sure to **find out the cutoff age for children's discounts.**

## Consulates

➤ CANADA: **Canadian Consulate** (Tal 29, tel. 089/219–9570).

➤ UNITED KINGDOM: **British Consulate General** (Bürkleinstr. 10, tel. 089/211–090).

➤ UNITED STATES: **U.S. Consulate General** (Königinstr. 5, tel. 089/28880).

## Consumer Protection

Whenever shopping or buying travel services in Germany, **pay with a major credit card** so you can cancel payment or get reimbursed if there's a problem. If you're buying a package or a tour, always **consider travel insurance** that includes default coverage (☞ Insurance, *below*).

➤ BBBS: **Council of Better Business Bureaus** (4200 Wilson Blvd., Suite 800, Arlington, VA 22203, tel. 703/276–0100, fax 703/525–8277 www.bbb.org).

## Customs & Duties

When shopping, **keep receipts** for all purchases. Upon reentering the country, **be ready to show customs officials what you've bought.** If you feel a duty is incorrect or object to the way your clearance was handled, note the inspector's badge number and ask to see a supervisor. If the problem isn't resolved, write to the appropriate authorities, beginning with the port director at your point of entry.

## IN GERMANY

Since a single, unrestricted market took effect within the European Union (EU) early in 1993, there have no longer been restrictions for persons traveling among the 15 EU countries. However, there are restrictions on what can be brought in without declaration.

For anyone entering Germany from outside the EU, the following limitations apply: (1) 200 cigarettes or 100 cigarillos or 50 cigars or 250 grams of tobacco; (2) 2 liters of still table wine; (3) 1 liter of spirits over 22% volume or 2 liters of spirits under 22% volume (fortified and sparkling wines) or 2 more liters of table wine; (4) 50 grams of perfume and 250 milliliters of toilet water; (5) other goods to the value of DM 350.

Tobacco and alcohol allowances are for visitors age 17 and over. Other items intended for personal use can be imported and exported freely. There are no restrictions on the import and export of German currency.

## IN AUSTRALIA

Australian residents 18 or older may bring home $A400 worth of souvenirs and gifts (including jewelry), 250 cigarettes or 250 grams of tobacco, and 1,125 milliliters of alcohol (including wine, beer, and spirits). Residents under 18 may bring back $A200 worth of goods. Prohibited items include meat products. Seeds, plants, and fruits need to be declared upon arrival.

➤ INFORMATION: **Australian Customs Service** (Regional Director, Box 8, Sydney, NSW 2001, tel. 02/9213–2000, fax 02/9213–4000).

## IN CANADA

Canadian residents who have been out of Canada for at least seven days may bring home C$500 worth of goods duty-free. If you've been away less than seven days but more than 48 hours, the duty-free allowance drops to C$200; if your trip lasts 24–48 hours, the allowance is C$50. You may not pool allowances with family members. Goods claimed under the C$500 exemption may follow you by mail; those claimed under the lesser exemptions must accompany you. Alcohol and tobacco products may be included in the seven-day and 48-hour exemptions but not in the 24-hour exemption. If you meet the age requirements of the province or territory through which you reenter Canada, you may bring in duty-free 1.14 liters (40 imperial ounces) of wine or liquor or 24 12-ounce cans or bottles of beer or ale. If you are 16 or older, you may bring in duty-free 200 cigarettes and 50 cigars. Check ahead of time with Revenue Canada or the Department of Agriculture for policies regarding meat products, seeds, plants, and fruits.

You may send an unlimited number of gifts worth up to C$60 each duty-free to Canada. Label the package UNSOLICITED GIFT— VALUE UNDER $60. Alcohol and tobacco are excluded.

➤ INFORMATION: **Revenue Canada** (2265 St. Laurent Blvd. S, Ottawa, Ontario K1G 4K3, tel. 613/993–0534; 800/461–9999 in Canada, fax 613/957–8911, www.ccra-adrc.gc.ca).

## IN NEW ZEALAND

Homeward-bound residents 17 or older may bring back $700 worth of souvenirs and gifts. Your duty-free allowance also includes 4.5 liters of wine or beer; one 1,125-milliliter bottle of spirits; and either 200 cigarettes, 250 grams of tobacco, 50 cigars, or a combination of the three up to 250 grams. Prohibited items include meat products, seeds, plants, and fruits.

➤ INFORMATION: **New Zealand Customs** (Custom House, 50 Anzac Ave., Box 29, Auckland, New Zealand, tel. 09/359–6655, fax 09/ 359–6732).

## IN THE U.K.

If you are a U.K. resident and your journey was wholly within the European Union (EU), you won't have to pass through customs when you return to the United Kingdom. If you plan to bring back large quantities of alcohol or tobacco, check EU limits beforehand.

➤ **Information: HM Customs and Excise** (Dorset House, Stamford St., Bromley, Kent BR1 1XX, tel. 020/7202–4227).

**IN THE U.S.**

U.S. residents who have been out of the country for at least 48 hours (and who have not used the $400 allowance or any part of it in the past 30 days) may bring home $400 worth of foreign goods duty-free.

U.S. residents 21 and older may bring back 1 liter of alcohol duty-free. In addition, regardless of your age, you are allowed 200 cigarettes and 100 non-Cuban cigars. Antiques, which the U.S. Customs Service defines as objects more than 100 years old, enter duty-free, as do original works of art done entirely by hand, including paintings, drawings, and sculptures.

You may also send packages home duty-free: up to $200 worth of goods for personal use, with a limit of one parcel per addressee per day (except alcohol or tobacco products or perfume worth more than $5); label the package PERSONAL USE and attach a list of its contents and their retail value. Do not label the package UNSOLICITED GIFT or your duty-free exemption will drop to $100. Mailed items do not affect your duty-free allowance on your return.

➤ **Information: U.S. Customs Service** (1300 Pennsylvania Ave. NW, Washington, DC 20229, www.customs.gov; inquiries tel. 202/354–1000; complaints c/o Office of Regulations and Rulings; registration of equipment c/o Resource Management, tel. 202/927–0540).

## Discounts & Deals

Be a smart shopper and **compare all your options** before making decisions. A plane ticket bought with a promotional coupon from travel clubs, coupon books, and direct-mail offers may not be cheaper than the least expensive fare from a discount ticket agency. And always keep in mind that what you get is just as important as what you save.

## DISCOUNT RESERVATIONS

To save money, **look into discount reservations services** with toll-free numbers, which use their buying power to get a better price on hotels, airline tickets, even car rentals. When booking a room, always **call the hotel's local toll-free number** (if one is available) rather than the central reservations number—you'll often get a better price. Always ask about special packages or corporate rates.

When shopping for the best deal on hotels and car rentals, **look for guaranteed exchange rates,** which protect you against a falling dollar. With your rate locked in, you won't pay more, even if the price goes up in the local currency.

➤ AIRLINE TICKETS: **tel. 800/FLY–4–LESS. tel. 800/FLY–ASAP.**

➤ HOTEL ROOMS: **International Marketing & Travel Concepts** (tel. 800/790–4682). **Steigenberger Reservation Service** (tel. 800/223–5652, www.srs-worldhotels.com). Travel Interlink (tel. 800/888–5898, www.travelinterlink.com).

## Electricity

To use your U.S.-purchased electric-powered equipment, **bring a converter and adapter.** The electrical current in Germany is 220 volts, 50 cycles alternating current (AC); wall outlets take Continental-type plugs, with two round prongs.

If your appliances are dual-voltage, you'll need only an adapter. Don't use 110-volt outlets, marked FOR SHAVERS ONLY, for high-wattage appliances such as blow-dryers. Most laptops operate equally well on 110 and 220 volts and so require only an adapter.

## Emergencies

➤ CONTACTS: **Police** (tel. 089/110). **Fire department, ambulance, and medical emergencies** (tel. 089/112).

## DOCTORS AND DENTISTS

The American, British, and Canadian consulates (☞ *above*) have lists of recommended doctors and dentists who speak English.

## PHARMACIES

Internationale Ludwigs-Apotheke, open weekdays 8–6 and Saturday 8–1, and Europa-Apotheke, open weekdays 8–6 and Saturday 8–1, stock a large variety of over-the-counter medications. Munich pharmacies stay open late on a rotating basis, and every pharmacy has a schedule in its window.

➤ **INFORMATION: Internationale Ludwigs-Apotheke** (Neuhauserstr. 11, tel. 089/260–3021). **Europa-Apotheke** (Schützenstr. 12, near the Hauptbahnhof, tel. 089/595–423).

# English-Language Bookstores

The Anglia English Bookshop is the leading English-language bookstore in Munich, although the shop is in incredible disorder. Hugendubel has a good selection as does The Internationale Presse store at the main train station and Words'worth, a well-kept shop.

➤ **INFORMATION: The Anglia English Bookshop** (Schellingstr. 3, tel. 089/283–642). **Hugendubel** (Marienpl. 22, 2nd floor, tel. 089/ 23890; Karlspl. 3, tel. 089/552–2530). **The Internationale Presse** (tel. 089/13080). **Words'worth** (Schellingstr. 21a, tel. 089/280– 9141).

# Guided Tours

## EXCURSIONS

Bus excursions to the Alps, to Austria, to the royal palaces and castles of Bavaria, or along the Romantic Road can be booked through DER, in the main train station. Next to the main train station, Panorama Tours operates numerous trips, including the Royal Castles Tour (Schlösserfahrt) of "Mad" King Ludwig's dream palaces; the cost is DM 78, excluding entrance fees to the palaces. Bookings for both companies can also be made through all major hotels in the city. The tours depart from in front of the Hauptbahnhof outside the Hertie department store.

➤ INFORMATION: **DER** (Hauptbahnhofpl. 2, in the main train station building, tel. 089/5514–0100). **Panorama Tours** (Arnulfstr. 8, tel. 089/5490–7560).

## ORIENTATION

A variety of city bus tours is offered by Panorama Tours. The blue buses operate year-round, departing from in front of the Hertie department store on Bahnhofplatz. A one-hour tour of Munich highlights leaves daily at 10, 11, 11:30, 12, 1, 2:30, 3, and 4. The cost is DM 17. A 2½-hour city tour departs daily at 10 AM and includes brief visits to the Alte Pinakothek, the Peterskirche, and Marienplatz for the glockenspiel. An afternoon tour, also 2½ hours and starting at 2:30 PM, includes a tour of Schloss Nymphenburg. The cost of each tour is DM 30. Another 2½-hour tour, departing Saturday, Sunday, and Monday at 10 AM, includes a visit to the Bavaria film studios. The cost is DM 39. A four-hour tour, starting daily at 10 AM and 2:30 PM includes a visit to the Olympic Park and the "Olympic Spirit" attraction. The cost is DM 49. The München bei Nacht tour provides 4½ hours of Munich by night and includes dinner and a show at the Hofbräuhaus, a trip up the Olympic Tower to admire the lights of the city, and a final drink in a nightclub. It departs April through November, Friday and Saturday at 7:30 PM; the cost is DM 100. Another operator, Yellow Cab Stadtrundfahrten, has a fleet of yellow double-decker buses, in which tours are offered simultaneously in eight languages. They leave hourly between 10 AM and 4 PM from in front of the Elisenhof shopping complex on Bahnhofplatz. A novel way of seeing the city is to hop on one of the bike-rickshaws which are the latest addition to the tour program. The bike-powered two-seater cabs operate between Marienplatz and the Chinesischer Turm in the Englischer Garten. Just hail one—or book ahead by calling 089/129–4808.

The Upper Bavarian Regional Tourist Office (☞ Visitor Information, *below*) provides information and brochures for excursions and accommodations outside Munich.

## WALKING AND BICYCLING

Downtown Munich is only a mile square and is easily explored on foot. Almost all the major attractions in the city center are on the interlinking web of pedestrian streets that run from Karlsplatz, by the main train station, to Marienplatz and the Viktualienmarkt and extend north around the Frauenkirche and up to Odeonsplatz. The two tourist information offices issue a free map with suggested walking tours (☞ Visitor Information, *below*).

Two-hour tours of the old city center are given daily in summer (March–October) and on Friday and Saturday in winter (November–February). Tours organized by the visitor center start at 10:30 and 1 in the center of Marienplatz. The cost is DM 16. Munich Walks conducts tours of the old city and sites related to the Third Reich era. The cost is DM 15 (DM 12 for under-26-year-olds, free for accompanied children under 14). Tours depart daily at 11 from the Hauptbahnhof, outside the EurAide office by Track 11. City Hopper Touren offers daily escorted bike tours March–October. Bookings must be made in advance, and starting times are negotiable. Radius Touristik has bicycle tours from May through the beginning of October at 10:15 and 2; the cost, including bike rental, is DM 15. Mike's Bike Tours is run by a young American who hires German students to take visitors on a two- to three-hour spin through Munich. The tours start daily at the Old Town Hall, the Altes Rathaus, at 11:20 and 3:50. They cost DM 28, including bike rental.

➤ BIKE TOURS: **City Hopper Touren** (tel. 089/272–1131). **Radius Touristik** (Arnulfstr. 3, opposite Platforms 30–36 in the Hauptbahnhof, tel. 089/596–113). **Mike's Bike Tours** (tel. 089/651–4275).

➤ WALKING TOURS: **Munich Walks** (tel. 0177/227–5901).

# Holidays

The following national holidays are observed in Munich: January 1; January 6 (Epiphany); April 13 (Good Friday); April 16 (Easter Monday); May 1 (Workers' Day); May 24 (Ascension); June 4 (Pentecost Monday); June 14 (Corpus Christi); August 15 (Assumption Day); October 3 (German Unity Day); November 1 (All Saints' Day); December 24–26 (Christmas).

# Insurance

The most useful travel insurance plan is a comprehensive policy that includes coverage for trip cancellation and interruption, default, trip delay, and medical expenses (with a waiver for preexisting conditions).

Without insurance you will lose all or most of your money if you cancel your trip, regardless of the reason. Default insurance covers you if your tour operator, airline, or cruise line goes out of business. Trip-delay covers expenses that arise because of bad weather or mechanical delays. Study the fine print when comparing policies.

For overseas travel, a key component of travel insurance is coverage for medical bills incurred if you get sick on the road. Such expenses are not generally covered by Medicare or private policies. U.K. residents can buy a travel insurance policy valid for most vacations taken during the year in which it's purchased (but check preexisting-condition coverage). British and Australian citizens need extra medical coverage when traveling overseas.

Always **buy travel policies directly from the insurance company**; if you buy them from a cruise line, airline, or tour operator that goes out of business, you probably will not be covered for the agency's or operator's default, a major risk. Before making any purchase, **review your existing health and home-owner's policies** to find what they cover away from home.

➤ TRAVEL INSURERS: In the U.S.: **Access America** (6600 W. Broad St., Richmond, VA 23230, tel. 804/285–3300 or 800/284–8300, fax 804/673–1583, www.previewtravel.com), **Travel Guard International** (1145 Clark St., Stevens Point, WI 54481, tel. 715/345–0505 or 800/826–1300, fax 800/955–8785, www.noelgroup.com). In Canada: **Voyager Insurance** (44 Peel Center Dr., Brampton, Ontario L6T 4M8, tel. 905/791–8700; 800/668–4342 in Canada).

➤ INSURANCE INFORMATION: In the U.K.: **Association of British Insurers** (51–55 Gresham St., London EC2V 7HQ, tel. 020/7600–3333, fax 020/7696–8999, www.abi.org.uk). In Australia: **Insurance Council of Australia** (tel. 03/9614–1077, fax 03/9614–7924).

## Language

The Germans are great linguists, and you'll find that English is spoken in most hotels, restaurants, airports, stations, museums, and other places of interest. However, English is not widely spoken in rural areas; this is especially true of the eastern part of Germany.

Unless you speak fluent German, you may find the regional dialect of Bavaria hard to follow. However most Germans can speak High or standard German.

## Lodging

The standards of German hotels are very high, down to the humblest inn. You can nearly always **expect courteous and polite service and clean and comfortable rooms.** In addition to hotels proper, the country has numerous *Gasthöfe* or *Gasthäuser*, which are country inns that serve food and also have rooms; pensions, or *Fremdenheime* (guest houses). Most hotels have restaurants, but those listed as *Garni* provide breakfast only. At the lowest end of the scale are *Fremdenzimmer*, meaning simply "rooms," normally in private houses.

**Ask about breakfast and bathing facilities** when booking. Room rates are by no means inflexible and depend very much on supply and demand. You can save money by inquiring about reductions. If you have booked and plan to arrive late, let the hotel know.

Tourist offices will also make bookings for a nominal fee, but they may have difficulty doing so after 4 PM in high season and on weekends, so **don't wait until too late in the day to begin looking for your accommodations.** If you do get stuck, ask someone—like a mail carrier, police officer, or waiter, for example—for directions to a house renting Fremdenzimmer or a Gasthof.

## HOSTELS

You can **save on lodging costs by staying at hostels.** In Bavaria, however, **there is an age limit of 27.** Germany's *Jugendherbergen* (youth hostels) are among the most efficient and up-to-date in Europe. In Germany you must be a member of a national hosteling association or Hostelling International (HI) in order to stay at a hostel. Membership in any HI national hostel association allows you to stay in HI-affiliated hostels at member rates (DM 20–DM 25).

➤ IN GERMANY: **DJH Service GmbH** (Postfach 1462, D–32704 Detmold, tel. 05231/74010, fax 05231/74010, www.djh.de).

➤ ORGANIZATIONS: **Hostelling International—American Youth Hostels** (733 15th St. NW, Suite 840, Washington, DC 20005, tel. 202/783–6161, fax 202/783–6171, www.hiayh.org). **Hostelling International—Canada** (400–205 Catherine St., Ottawa, Ontario K2P 1C3, tel. 613/237–7884, fax 613/237–7868, www.hostellingintl.ca). **Youth Hostel Association of England and Wales** (Trevelyan House, 8 St. Stephen's Hill, St. Albans, Hertfordshire AL1 2DY, tel. 01727/855215 or 01727/845047, fax 01727/844126, www.yha.uk). **Australian Youth Hostel Association** (10 Mallett St., Camperdown, NSW 2050, tel. 02/9565–1699, fax 02/9565–1325, www.yha.com.au). **Youth Hostels Association of New Zealand** (Box 436, Christchurch,

New Zealand, tel. 03/379-9970, fax 03/365-4476, www.yha.org.nz).

## Mail

### POSTAL RATES

Airmail letters to the United States and Canada cost DM 3; postcards, DM 2. All letters to the United Kingdom cost DM 1.10; postcards, DM 1.

### RECEIVING MAIL

You can arrange to have mail sent to you in care of any German post office; **have the envelope marked "Postlagernd."** This service is free. Or you can have mail sent to any American Express office in Germany. There's no charge to cardholders, holders of American Express traveler's checks, or anyone who has booked a vacation with American Express.

## Money Matters

### ATMS

Twenty-four-hour ATMs (Geldautomaten) can be accessed with PLUS or Cirrus credit and banking cards. Some German banks exact DM4–DM10 fees for use of their ATMs. Your PIN number should be set for four digits; if it's longer, ask your bank about changing it for your trip. Since some ATM keypads show no letters, know the numeric equivalent of your password.

### CREDIT CARDS

All major U.S. credit cards are accepted in Germany. If you get a four-digit PIN number for your card before you leave home, you can use your credit card at German ATMs.

Throughout this guide the following abbreviations are used: **AE,** American Express; **DC,** Diner's Club; **MC,** MasterCard; and **V,** Visa.

### CURRENCY

This is the last year of the Deutschmark. Both D-marks and euros can be used until July 1, 2002, when the euro takes over.

During the transition you may get your change in euros even if you pay in marks. Stores, restaurants, and other businesses nearly always show their prices in both the D-mark and the euro. The mark is divided into 100 pfennige. There are bills of 5 (rare), 10, 20, 50, 100, 200, 500, and 1,000 marks and coins of 1, 2, 5, 10, and 50 pfennige and 1, 2, and 5 marks. At press time, the mark stood at DM 2.32 to the U.S. dollar, 1.51 to the Canadian dollar, 3.37 to the British pound sterling, and DM 1.21 to the Australian dollar.

## CURRENCY EXCHANGE

For the most favorable rates, **change money through banks.** Although ATM transaction fees may be higher abroad than at home, ATM rates are excellent because they are based on wholesale rates offered only by major banks. You won't do as well at exchange booths in airports or rail and bus stations, in hotels, in restaurants, or in stores. To avoid lines at airport exchange booths, **get a bit of local currency before you leave home.**

➤ EXCHANGE SERVICES: **International Currency Express** (tel. 888/278–6628 for orders, www.foreignmoney.com). **Thomas Cook Currency Services** (tel. 800/287–7362 for telephone orders and retail locations, www.us.thomascook.com).

## TRAVELER'S CHECKS

Lost or stolen checks can usually be replaced within 24 hours. To ensure a speedy refund, buy your own traveler's checks—don't let someone else pay for them: irregularities like this can cause delays. The person who bought the checks should make the call to request a refund.

# Packing

What you pack depends more on the time of year than on any particular dress code. Winters can be bitterly cold; summers are warm but with days that suddenly turn cool and rainy. In summer **take a warm jacket or heavy sweater** for the Bavarian Alps, where the nights can be chilly even after hot days.

**Pack as you would for an American city:** dressy outfits for formal restaurants and nightclubs, casual clothes elsewhere. Jeans are as popular in Germany as anywhere else and are perfectly acceptable for sightseeing and informal dining. In the evening men will probably feel more comfortable wearing a jacket and tie in more expensive restaurants, although it is almost never required. Many German women are extremely fashion-conscious and wear stylish outfits to restaurants and the theater.

To discourage purse snatchers and pickpockets, **carry a handbag with long straps** that you can sling across your body bandolier style and with a zippered compartment for money and other valuables.

In your carry-on luggage **bring an extra pair of eyeglasses or contact lenses** and **enough of any medication you take** to last the entire trip. You may also want your doctor to write a spare prescription using the drug's generic name, since brand names may vary from country to country. In luggage to be checked, **never pack prescription drugs or valuables.** To avoid customs delays, carry medications in their original packaging.

## CHECKING LUGGAGE

How many carry-on bags you can bring with you is up to the airline. Most allow two but not always, so make sure that everything you carry aboard will fit under your seat or in the overhead bin, and get to the gate early.

Before departure, **itemize your bags' contents** and their worth, and label the bags with your name, address, and phone number (if you use your home address, cover it so potential thieves can't see it readily). Inside each bag, **pack a copy of your itinerary.** At check-in, **make sure that each bag is correctly tagged** with the destination airport's three-letter code. If your bags arrive damaged or fail to arrive at all, file a written report with the airline before leaving the airport.

## Passports & Visas

When traveling internationally, **carry your passport even if you don't need one** (it's always the best form of ID) and **make two photocopies of the data page** (one for someone at home and another for you, carried separately from your passport). If you lose your passport, promptly call the nearest embassy or consulate and the local police.

### ENTERING GERMANY

U.S., Canadian, and British citizens need only a valid passport to enter Germany for stays of up to 90 days.

### PASSPORT OFFICES

➤ AUSTRALIAN CITIZENS: **Australian Passport Office** (tel. 131–232, www.dfat.gov.au/passports).

➤ CANADIAN CITIZENS: **Passport Office** (tel. 819/994–3500 or 800/567–6868, www.dfait-maeci.gc.ca/passport).

➤ NEW ZEALAND CITIZENS: **New Zealand Passport Office** (tel. 04/494–0700, www.passports.govt.nz).

➤ U.K. CITIZENS: **London Passport Office** (tel. 0990/210–410) for fees and documentation requirements and to request an emergency passport.

➤ U.S. CITIZENS: **National Passport Information Center** (tel. 900/225–5674; calls are 35¢ per minute for automated service, $1.05 per minute for operator service).

## Public Transportation

Munich has an efficient and well-integrated public transportation system, consisting of the U-bahn (subway), the S-bahn (suburban railway), the Strassenbahn (streetcars), and buses. Marienplatz forms the heart of the U-bahn and S-bahn network, which operates from around 5 AM to 1 AM. An all-night tram and bus service operates on main routes within the city. For a clear explanation in English of how the system works, pick up a copy of *Rendezvous mit München*, available free of charge at all tourist offices.

Fares are uniform for the entire system. As long as you are traveling in the same direction, you can transfer from one mode of transportation to another on the same ticket. You can also interrupt your journey as often as you like, and time-punched tickets are valid for up to four hours, depending on the number of zones you travel through. Fares are constantly creeping upward, but at press time a basic Einzelfahrkarte (one-way ticket) cost DM 3.60 for a ride in the inner zone and DM 1.80 for a short journey of up to four stops. If you're taking a number of trips around the city, save money by buying a Mehrfahrtenkarte, or multiple strip ticket. Red strip tickets are valid for children under 15 only. Blue strips cover adults. DM 15 buys a 10-strip ticket. All but the shortest inner-area journeys (up to four stops) cost two strips (one for young people between 15 and 21), which must be validated at one of the many time-punching machines at stations or on buses and trams.

For a short stay the best option is the Tageskarte ticket, which provides unlimited travel for up to five people (maximum of two adults, plus three children under 15). It is valid weekdays from 9 AM to 6 AM the following day and at any time on weekends. The costs are DM 13 for an inner-zone ticket and DM 26 for the entire network. The Welcome Card covers transport within the city boundaries and includes up to 50% reductions in admission to many museums and attractions. The card, obtainable from visitor information offices, costs DM 12 for one day and DM 29 for three days. A three-day card for two people costs DM 42.

All tickets are sold at the blue dispensers at U- and S-bahn stations and at bus and streetcar stops. Bus and streetcar drivers, all tourist offices, and Mehrfahrtenkarten booths (which display a white κ on a green background) also sell tickets. Spot checks are common and carry an automatic fine of DM 60 if you're caught without a valid ticket. Holders of a EurailPass, a Youth Pass or an Inter-Rail card can travel free on all suburban railway trains.

## Senior-Citizen Travel

To qualify for age-related discounts, **mention your senior-citizen status up front** when booking hotel reservations (not when checking out). When renting a car, ask about promotional car-rental discounts, which can be cheaper than senior-citizen rates. Also take advantage of discounts on railway tickets and reduced admission to museums. Contact the German National Tourist Office (☞ Visitor Information, *below*).

➤ Educational Programs: **Elderhostel** (75 Federal St., 3rd floor, Boston, MA 02110, tel. 877/426–8056, fax 877/426–2166, www.elderhostel.org). **Interhostel** (University of New Hampshire, 6 Garrison Ave., Durham, NH 03824, tel. 603/862–1147 or 800/733–9753, fax 603/862–1113, www.learn.unh.edu).

## Students in Germany

Most museums and modes of transportation have reduced prices for students, so have your student ID card handy. *See* Lodging, *above,* for hostelling information.

➤ IDs & Services: **Council Travel** (CIEE; 205 E. 42nd St., 14th floor, New York, NY 10017, tel. 212/822–2700 or 888/268–6245, fax 212/822–2699, www.councilexchanges.org), for mail orders only (in the United States). **Travel Cuts** (187 College St., Toronto, Ontario M5T 1P7, tel. 416/979–2406 or 800/667–2887, www.travelcuts.com), in Canada.

## Taxes

### VALUE-ADDED TAX

Most prices you see on items already have Germany's 16% value-added tax (VAT) included. When traveling to a non-EU country, you are entitled to a refund of the VAT you pay (multiply the price of an item by 13.8% to find out how much VAT is embedded in the price). Some goods, like books and antiquities, carry a 6.5% VAT as a percentage of the purchase price.

Global Refund is a VAT refund service that makes getting your money back hassle-free. The service is available Europe-wide at 130,000 affiliated stores. In participating stores, **ask for the Global Refund form** (called a Shopping Cheque). If a store is not a participating member of Global Refund, they'll probably have a form called an *Ausfuhr-Abnehmerbescheinigung*, which Global Refund can also process, for a higher fee. When you leave the European Union, you must be prepared **show your purchases to customs officials** before they will stamp your refund form. You might not be permitted to carry these purchases in carry-on luggage, so **pack the items so that they are easily reached in your check-in luggage.** Before you check your luggage at the airport, **ask to be directed to the customs desk.** At Munich's airport, there are VAT refund counters between the areas of B and C, as well as between C and D. Once the form is stamped, take it to one of the more than 700 Global Refund counters— conveniently located at every major airport and border crossing—and your money will be refunded on the spot in the form of cash, check, or a refund to your credit-card account (minus a small percentage for processing). Alternatively, you can mail your validated form to Global Refund.

➤ **VAT Refunds: Global Refund** (707 Summer St., Stamford, CT 06901, tel. 800/566–9828, fax 203/674–8709, www.globalrefund.com).

## Taxis

Munich's cream-color taxis are numerous. Hail them in the street or call 089/21610 (there's an extra charge of DM 2 if you call). Rates start at DM 5. Expect to pay DM 12–DM 13 for a short trip within the city. There is a DM 1 charge for each piece of luggage.

# Telephones

### AREA & COUNTRY CODES

The country code for Germany is 49. When dialing a German number from abroad, drop the initial 0 from the local area code.

### DIRECTORY & OPERATOR ASSISTANCE

The German telephone system is fully automatic, and it's unlikely you'll have to employ the services of an operator unless you're seeking information. If you have difficulty reaching your number, call 0180/200–1033. You can book collect calls through this number to the United States but not to other countries. For information dial 11833 for numbers within Germany and 11834 for numbers elsewhere. International operators speak English.

### INTERNATIONAL CALLS

International calls can be made from just about any telephone booth in Germany. It costs only 48 pfennigs per minute to call the United States, day or night. Use a phone card or make international calls from post offices. You pay the clerk the cost of the call plus a DM 2 connection fee. At a hotel, rates will be at least double the regular charge, so **never make international calls from your room.**

### LOCAL CALLS

A local call from a telephone booth costs 30 pfennigs and will last for six minutes.

### LONG-DISTANCE SERVICES

AT&T, MCI, and Sprint access codes make calling long distance relatively convenient, but you may find the local access number blocked in many hotel rooms. First ask the hotel operator to connect you. If the hotel operator balks, ask for an international operator, or dial the international operator yourself.

➤ ACCESS CODES: In Germany: **AT&T Direct** (tel. 0130–0010 or 0800/ 225–5288). **MCI WorldCom** (tel. 0130–0012). **Sprint** (tel. 0130– 0013).

## PUBLIC PHONES

Most telephone booths in Germany now are card-operated, and it's risky to assume you'll find a coin-operated booth when you need one, so **buy a phone card.** You can purchase one at any German post office (also available at many exchange places). They come in denominations of DM 12 and DM 50, the latter good for DM 60 worth of calls. Most phone booths have instructions in English as well as German. Another advantage of the card: it charges only what the call cost. Coin-operated phones, which take 10-pfennig, DM 1, and DM 5 coins, don't make change.

## Tipping

The service charges on bills is sufficient for most tips in your hotel, though you should **tip bellhops and porters**; DM 2 per bag or service is ample. It's also customary to leave a small tip (a couple of marks per night) for the room-cleaning staff. Whether you tip the desk clerk depends on whether he or she has given you any special service.

Service charges are included in all restaurant checks (listed as *Bedienung*), as is tax (listed as MWST). Nonetheless, it is customary to **round up the bill to the nearest mark or to leave about 5%** (give it to the waiter or waitress as you pay the bill; don't leave it on the table, as that's considered rude). Bartenders and servers also expect a 2–5% tip.

In taxis **round up the fare a couple of marks** as a tip. Only give more if you have particularly cumbersome or heavy luggage (though you will be charged 50 pfennigs for each piece of luggage anyway).

## Tours & Packages

Because everything is prearranged on a prepackaged tour or independent vacation, you'll spend less time planning—and often get it all at a good price.

## BOOKING WITH AN AGENT

Travel agents are excellent resources. But it's a good idea to collect brochures from several agencies as some agents' suggestions may be influenced by relationships with tour and package firms that reward them for volume sales. If you have a special interest, **find an agent with expertise in that area**; ASTA (☞ Travel Agencies, *below*) has a database of specialists worldwide.

Make sure your travel agent knows the accommodations and other services of the place they're recommending. Ask about the hotel's location, room size, beds, and whether it has a pool, room service, or programs for children, if you care about these. Has your agent been there in person or sent others whom you can contact?

Do some homework on your own, too: local tourism boards can provide information about lesser-known and small-niche operators, some of which may sell only direct.

## BUYER BEWARE

Each year consumers are stranded or lose their money when tour operators—even large ones with excellent reputations—go out of business. So **check out the operator.** Ask several travel agents about its reputation and try to **book with a company that has a consumer-protection program** (look for information in the company's brochure). In the United States members of the National Tour Association and the United States Tour Operators Association are required to set aside funds to cover your payments and travel arrangements in the event that the company defaults. It's also a good idea to choose a company that participates in the American Society of Travel Agents' Tour Operator Program (TOP); ASTA will act as mediator in any disputes between you and your tour operator.

Remember that the more your package or tour includes, the better you can predict the ultimate cost of your vacation. Make sure you know exactly what is covered and **beware of hidden costs.** Are taxes, tips, and transfers included? Entertainment and excursions? These can add up.

➤ TOUR-OPERATOR RECOMMENDATIONS: **American Society of Travel Agents** (☞ Travel Agencies, below). **National Tour Association** (NTA; 546 E. Main St., Lexington, KY 40508, tel. 606/226–4444 or 800/682–8886, www.ntaonline.com). **United States Tour Operators Association** (USTOA; 342 Madison Ave., Suite 1522, New York, NY 10173, tel. 212/599–6599 or 800/468–7862, fax 212/599–6744, www.ustoa.com).

## Train Travel

All long-distance rail services arrive at and depart from the Hauptbahnhof, the main train station; trains to and from some destinations in Bavaria use the adjoining Starnbergerbahnhof, which is under the same roof. The high-speed InterCity Express (ICE) trains connect Munich, Augsburg, Frankfurt, and Hamburg on one line; Munich, Nuremberg, Würzburg, and Hamburg on another. Regensburg can be reached from Munich on Regio trains. For information on train schedules, call 01805–9966333; most railroad information staff speak English. For tickets and travel information, go to the station information office or try the ABR travel agency, right by the station on Bahnhofplatz.

## Travel Agencies

A good travel agent puts your needs first. Look for an agency that has been in business at least five years, emphasizes customer service, and has someone on staff who specializes in your destination. In addition, **make sure the agency belongs to a professional trade organization.** The American Society of Travel Agents (ASTA), with 27,000 agents in some 170 countries, is the largest and most influential in the field. Operating under the motto "Integrity in Travel," it maintains and enforces a strict code of ethics and will step in to help mediate any agent-client disputes if necessary. ASTA also maintains a Web site that includes a directory of agents. (If a travel agency is also acting as your tour operator, *see* Buyer Beware in Tours & Packages, *above*.)

➤ **LOCAL AGENT REFERRALS: American Society of Travel Agents** (ASTA; tel. 800/965–2782 24-hr hot line, fax 703/684–8319, www.astanet.com). **Association of British Travel Agents** (68–71 Newman St., London W1P 4AH, tel. 020/7637–2444, fax 020/7637–0713, www.abtanet.com). **Association of Canadian Travel Agents** (1729 Bank St., Suite 201, Ottawa, Ontario K1V 7Z5, tel. 613/521–0474, fax 613/521–0805). **Australian Federation of Travel Agents** (Level 3, 309 Pitt St., Sydney 2000, tel. 02/9264–3299, fax 02/9264–1085, www.afta.com.au). **Travel Agents' Association of New Zealand** (Box 1888, Wellington 10033, tel. 04/499–0104, fax 04/499–0827).

➤ **WITHIN MUNICH: American Express** (Promenadenpl. 6, tel. 089/290–900). **DER** (Bahnhofpl. 2, tel. 089/5514–0100) and at the Münchner-Freiheit Square, in Schwabing (Münchner-Freiheit 6, tel. 089/336–033).

## Visitor Information

The monthly English-language magazine *Munich Found* is sold at most newspaper stands and in many hotels. Munich has two tourist information offices, at the Hauptbahnhof and at the Info-Service in the Rathaus, open weekdays 10–8, Sat. 10–4.

➤ **BAVARIAN MOUNTAIN REGION: Tourismusverband München-Oberbayern** (Upper Bavarian Regional Tourist Office; Bodenseestr. 113, D–81243, tel. 089/829–180).

➤ **MUNICH TOURIST OFFICES: Hauptbahnhof** (Bahnhofpl. 2, next to DER travel agency, tel. 089/2303–0300, www.munich-tourist.de). **Info-Service** (Marienpl., tel. 089/2332–8242).

➤ **GERMAN NATIONAL TOURIST OFFICE: U.S. Nationwide** (122 E. 42nd St., New York, NY 10168, tel. 212/661–7200, fax 212/661–7174). **Canada** (175 Bloor St. E, Suite 604, Toronto, Ontario M4W 3R8, tel. 416/968–1570, fax 416/968–1986). **U.K.** (18 Conduit St.,

London W1R ODT, tel. 020/7317–0908, fax 020/7495–6129).
**Australia** (Box A980, Sydney, NSW 1235, tel. 9267–8148, fax
9267–9035).

## When to Go

### CLIMATE

Germany's climate is temperate and the south is normally a few
degrees warmer than the north, although cold spells can plunge
the thermometer well below freezing in the Bavarian Alps, just
south of Munich. The sunny and warm days of summer set in
around May, though you should **be prepared for a few cloudy
and wet days.** Fall is sometimes spectacular here—warm and
soothing. The weather can be strikingly variable in southern
Bavaria due to the Föhn, an Alpine wind that gives rise to clear but
very warm conditions. The Föhn can occur in all seasons. Sudden
atmospheric pressure changes associated with the Föhn give
some people headaches. Germans measure temperature in
Celsius, not Fahrenheit. For example, 23.9°C is a pleasant day of
75°F; 10°C is a chilly 50°F.

➤ FORECASTS: The following are the average daily maximum and
minimum temperatures for Munich.

**MUNICH**

| Jan. | 35F | 1C | May | 64F | 18C | Sept. | 67F | 20C |
|------|-----|----|-----|-----|-----|-------|-----|-----|
| | 23 | − 5 | | 45 | 7 | | 48 | 9 |
| Feb. | 38F | 3C | June | 70F | 21C | Oct. | 56F | 14C |
| | 23 | − 5 | | 51 | 11 | | 40 | 4 |
| Mar. | 48F | 9C | July | 74F | 23C | Nov. | 44F | 7C |
| | 30 | − 1 | | 55 | 13 | | 33 | 0 |
| Apr. | 56F | 14C | Aug. | 73F | 23C | Dec. | 36F | 2C |
| | 38 | 3 | | 54 | 12 | | 26 | − 4 |

# INDEX